CHOSEN by Grace

Also by Stuart Tyner

Searching for the God of Grace

The ABZs of Adventist Youth Ministry

The Colors of Grace in Our Homes: 100 Creative Ideas to Enrich Family Worship

Summer Ministries: How to Revolutionize Your Town with Targeted Project Evangelism

Walking on the Edge: Thirteen Interactive Bible Studies for Adventist Students in Public High School

STUART TYNER

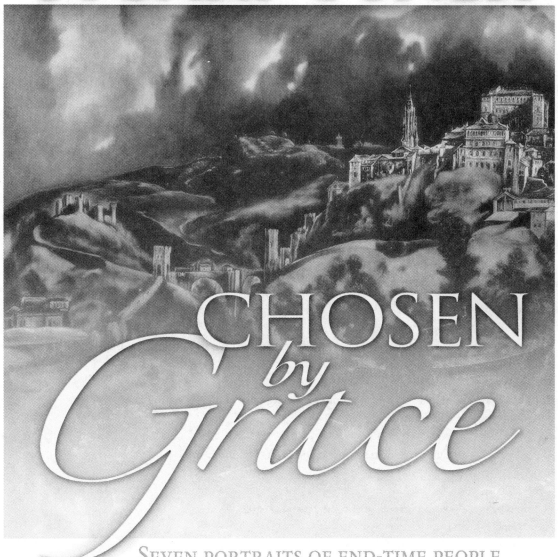

CHOSEN by Grace

SEVEN PORTRAITS OF END-TIME PEOPLE

PACIFIC PRESS® PUBLISHING ASSOCIATION
NAMPA, IDAHO
OSHAWA, ONTARIO, CANADA
WWW.PACIFICPRESS.COM

Cover design by Steve Lanto
Cover art by artist El Greco *Thunderstorm at Toledo*
Inside design by Aaron Troia

You can obtain additional copies of this book by calling toll-free 1-800-765-6955 or by visiting www.adventistbookcenter.com.

Library of Congress Cataloging-in-Publication Data:

Tyner, Stuart, 1946–
  Chosen by grace : seven portraits of end-time people / Stuart Tyner.
    p. cm.
  ISBN 13: 978-0-8163-2309-8 (paperback)
  ISBN 10: 0-8163-2309-7 (paperback)
  1. Grace (Theology) 2. Eschatology. 3. Seventh-day
Adventists—Doctrines. I. Title.
  BT761.3.T958   2009
  234—dc22
                                                    2009012783

09 10 11 12 13 • 5 4 3 2 1

DEDICATION

To Erin Noelle,
from the highest mountaintops
through the deepest valleys
clinging to grace

CONTENTS

ACKNOWLEDGMENTS

There are so many to whom I am thankful for their encouragement, their helpful reflections, and their supportive conversations as *Chosen by Grace* has emerged. First of all, as always, I am thankful to Karen, who not only put up with my late night and early morning study and creating sessions but, in the process of this project, has also proved to be the most valuable spiritual resource. The passages in this manuscript from *The Message* Bible have virtually all come from Karen because she knows that Bible so well and she so easily sees the benefit of fresh, contemporary expressions of God's timeless Word. Here's to another forty-two years together!

And again, as with *Searching for the God of Grace,* a hearty thanks to the dear friends who meet each week in study at our house. Thank you to Karen, Josh Anguiano, Lorelei and Peter Cress, Ryan and Sharilyn Horner, Jeff and Stefani McFarland, Patti Johnson, Jennifer Renaud, J'Leen Saeger, Debbie and Tom Saknit, Jenni Subriar, and Corey Swenson. You have again been willing to read a manuscript line by line, chapter by chapter (here a little, there a little!), looking for the good parts, editing to make the presentation more clear and consistent, discussing the historical and biblical content, and helping me make the relevant applications. Your continual growth in grace has inspired me. Your determination to find Jesus in every spiritual subject, even the most difficult ones like the end of time and the remnant, has motivated me. Let's keep studying together.

Thank you, too, to our dear New Zealand family and colleagues at the Papatoetoe Adventist church in Auckland: Brigette and Warwick Bagg, Keira Bullock, Virginia Christensen, Leanne and Stephen Davies, Hayley Duncan and Ronnie Davidson, Jacinda and Rick Harman, Liz and Norm Hurlow, Robert and Christina Levi, Keryn and Ryan McCutcheon, Christine Miles, Karyn and Richard Newson, and Emma Weslake. We have discussed these topics together around the staff table at your church; while traveling together in Egypt, Jordan, and Israel; and here in southern California. Our explorations of the settings of the biblical stories led us all to appreciate more fully the great themes of the Bible and to identify more closely with the Bible characters. I love the work you are doing at the PAPSDA church. Always model your leadership after Jesus and stay centered in His grace.

To Wayne French, the creative and constant chaplain of Avondale College in Australia, thanks not only for your love of grace, but also for already setting aside a week next year so we can together lead a discussion of the themes of this book with your students at another Festival of Faith. You are an inspiration to me.

And to my growing group of friends at Pacific Press in Idaho, thank you for your welcome and warmth during this year's Spiritual Emphasis week, for your enthusiastic acceptance of approaching the end times from a grace orientation, and for the creative ways you publish the good news. Thanks especially to the superb editor and kindred spirit David Jarnes; I have now had two remarkable experiences of working on a manuscript with David, and no one appreciates his work more than I.

May it be the experience of us all to continue to "grow in the grace and knowledge of our Lord and Savior Jesus Christ. To him be glory both now and forever! Amen" (2 Peter 3:18).

IN PURSUIT OF THE MYSTIC LAMB

Is it possible to be outwardly religious and actively orthodox and yet miss what is essential to a fulfilling life of faith? Can two people pursue the same spiritual goal yet arrive at diametrically opposing places? Can we Christians even miss altogether what is absolutely central to Christianity?

In the gloomy European spring of 1940, the frightened mayor of Ghent in Belgium asked the French government for a favor. The request had to do with an exceptional piece of art that hung in Saint Bavo's Cathedral in the mayor's city. Completed in 1432 by the extraordinary Flemish artist Jan van Eyck, the painting, on twenty-four oak panels, has been called the single finest work ever created in all of Western civilization. Officially, the celebrated art treasure is known as the *Ghent Altarpiece,* but most people call it the Adoration of the Mystic Lamb, after the glorious symbolic central panel, which depicts the worship of Jesus, the Lamb of God who takes away the sin of the world.

The mayor asked if he could entrust this deeply spiritual altarpiece to the French for safekeeping. The French accepted the assignment, received the altarpiece secretly, and on the sixteenth of May 1940, moved it from Paris to an undisclosed chateau in Pau in southern France, where it remained hidden until late summer 1942. Then, suddenly, a dangerous turn of events placed the Adoration of the Mystic Lamb in a perilous position.

In those dark days in the late 1930s and early 1940s, two groups of people had emerged in Europe. They pursued similar goals but from perspectives that were poles apart and contradictory. The people in both groups loved art, and their preferences were for the Western tradition: the classic Greek vases and Roman sculptures; the ornate devotional art of medieval times; the magnificent accomplishments of the Renaissance by such giants as Leonardo da Vinci, Michelangelo, and Raphael; the masterful European art of the seventeenth century—especially art from northern Europe (Rubens, Rembrandt, and Vermeer); the elegant, neoclassical eighteenth-century works; and the delightful interpretations of the impressionists from the end of the nineteenth century. Both groups collected the art they loved, sometimes privately accumulating one or two pieces and sometimes amassing vast numbers of treasures to stock imposing state museums.

The first group admired art for three primary reasons: they appreciated the beauty that art brought into their lives; they celebrated the talent that so skillfully reproduced scenes of local charm and settings of biblical, historical, and mythical significance; and they recognized the priceless value of the works produced by the great painters.

The second group shared these three attributes but added one more dynamic to their pursuit of art. In addition to their high regard of beauty, skill, and value, they also believed that the pleasures of art were *owed* to them. Author Edward Dolnick writes of art collectors who imagined that a piece of quality art "advertised its owner's merits." These collectors convinced themselves that they *deserved* to be rewarded with beautiful art because they were a superior people, a higher quality of men and women than their inferior neighbors— a master race who could take whatever they wanted wherever they found it and make it their own.

The first group was made up of people who simply loved art. The second group we know as Nazis. They were avid pillagers of other people's possessions—plunderers of personal and state-owned collections of art. They committed unspeakable crimes in the pursuit of their mission. No cruel or inhuman behavior was beneath their depraved capability. No bribe was too costly for their bloated state coffers. No locally revered "national treasure" was beyond their covetous grasp. No individual was so important

Jan van Eyck, *Ghent Altarpiece* (Adoration of the Mystic Lamb)
To view this painting in color, go to www.pacificpress.com/chosenbygrace.

or powerful as to be able to stop them. The Nazis exterminated millions of people, and along the way they grabbed all the precious art they could get their hands on.

Under pressure from the Germans, Vichy Prime Minister Pierre Laval issued an order on August 3, 1942, permitting the removal of the *Ghent Altarpiece* from its hiding place in Pau. Vehicles belonging to a professional transport firm from Munich, the *Spedition Wetsch,* rolled onto the chateau premises and the confiscated artwork was loaded onto them. The Vichy militia escorted the caravan as it made its way to Germany by way of Bordeaux, Tours, Dijon, and Belfort.

The first stop in Germany was Neuschwanstein, "mad" King Ludwig's legendary, theatrical castle in southwest Bavaria that became the inspiration for the Sleeping Beauty Castle in Disneyland. The altarpiece was kept in storage in the castle along with more than twenty-one thousand other pieces of art plundered almost entirely from French Jews. The stolen artwork usually arrived in Germany on one of Hermann Goering's private trains. In one such shipment on February 3, 1941, the cargo included forty-two crates filled with the Rothschilds' art treasures. This enormously wealthy banking family had amassed one of the most prestigious private collections of all time. Among the 5,009 works of art stolen by Goering and shipped to Germany were paintings by Leonardo da Vinci, Raphael, Rubens, Titian, Goya, and Ingres, and, in crate H13, marked with a swastika and destined for Adolph Hitler himself, *The Astronomer* by Vermeer.

In the summer of 1944, with the war effort deteriorating on all fronts for the Germans, the Adoration of the Mystic Lamb was transferred to the cold caverns of a deep, abandoned salt mine near Altaussee, Austria. There the Nazis safeguarded the works destined to be transported to Hitler's hometown of Linz and placed in the *Führermuseum,* which Hitler dreamed would become the greatest art museum in the entire world. The Nazis hid 6,577 paintings, 2,300 drawings and watercolors, 954 prints, 137 sculptures, and hundreds of cases with other art objects in the mine.

However, by the spring of 1945, Germany's last hopes for victory had died, and the defeated German armed forces were in retreat. One night early in May, a morose Nazi officer in charge of the salt-mine treasures announced that he had positioned sticks of dynamite throughout the entire collection, intending to "blow it all to bits" the next day rather than allow it to fall back into the hands of "world Jewry." Other officers, stunned by the thought of the destruction of all that priceless art, realized they must frustrate this "insane plan." On the morning of May 8, they arrested the officer and shortly thereafter informed the Allies of the presence of the works of art.

American military engineers defused the explosives. Half a mile down a long tunnel, through massive iron doors that had been kept padlocked, the Americans found the panels of the *Ghent Altarpiece* lying on top of four empty cardboard boxes.

Art lovers and Nazis. On the surface, two groups driven by a similar interest. Both valued art. Both collected art. Both were in determined pursuit of the Mystic Lamb. But beneath the outward similarities were embedded deeply significant and consequential distinctions.

THE BIBLE'S STORY OF CONTRASTING GROUPS

The Bible insists that at the end of time on planet Earth there will be only two groups of people. The first group accepts Christ's gift of eternal salvation, choosing to spend eternity with Him. The second group chooses instead to perish in the lake of fire. The same Bible that promises us that an innumerable host "from every nation, tribe, people and language" will be eternally saved (Revelation 7:9) also reveals that another group, as numerous as the "sand on the seashore" (20:8), will refuse the gift of salvation.

The biblical contrast between the two groups is stark: wise and foolish (Matthew 25:2). Sheep and goats (25:31–33). The righteous and the wicked (13:47–50). The children of light and the children of darkness (Ephesians 5:8). Those who overcome the "great dragon" (Revelation 12:9–11), and those who worship the beast (14:9, 10). Those who "follow the Lamb wherever He goes" (14:4), and those who "make war against the Lamb" (17:14). Those "whose names are written in the Lamb's book of life" (21:27), and those who names are blotted out (3:5).

The writers of Scripture have taken great care to name these two groups and classify them in symbolical terms. Might the Bible then also reveal the characteristics that distinguish one group from the other? Is there anything in all the Bible passages about the end of human history that would help us discover what qualities are held in common by the group to which we so desire to belong—those who choose to stand with the Lamb on Mount Zion (14:1)?

In the following seven chapters, we'll find that the answer definitely is Yes! We *can* know who the followers of the Lamb really are. In this study, we'll refer to them as "end-time people" and "the final remnant." And we'll contrast the characteristics of this group with the characteristics of the group whose fiery future is, to this very moment, still avoidable: " 'Even now,' declares the LORD, 'return to me with all your heart' " (Joel 2:12).

The Mystic Lamb still is calling His people to come out of that vast second group and join Him in worship now and for eternity (Revelation 18:4).[1]

---

1. You can read more about the stealing of European art by the Nazis and about its recovery in the following excellent books: Edward Dolnick, *The Forger's Spell: A True Story of Vermeer, Nazis, and the Greatest Art Hoax of the Twentieth Century* (New York: HarperCollins, 2008); Robert Edsel, *Rescuing Da Vinci: Hitler and the Nazis Stole Europe's Great Art—America and Her Allies Recovered It* (Dallas: Laurel Publishing, LLC, 2006); Hector Feliciano, *The Lost Museum: The Nazi Conspiracy to Steal the World's Greatest Works of Art* (New York: HarperCollins, 1997); Lynn Nicholas, *The Rape of Europa: The Fate of Europe's Treasures in the Third Reich and the Second World War* (New York: Random House, 1994); Jonathan Petropoulos, *The Faustian Bargain: The Art World in Nazi Germany* (Oxford: Oxford University Press, 2000).

"Art can teach (and much great art deliberately sets out to do so) without at all ceasing to be art."

—C. S. Lewis, *Letters of C. S. Lewis*

"We are, not metaphorically but in very truth, a Divine work of art, something that God is making, and therefore something with which He will not be satisfied until it has a certain character. . . .

"Over a sketch made idly to amuse a child, an artist may not take much trouble; he may be content to let it go even though it is not exactly as he meant it to be. But over the great picture of his life—the work which he loves, though in a different fashion, as intensely as a man loves a woman or a mother a child—he will take endless trouble."

—C. S. Lewis, *The Problem of Pain*

VISION NUMBER ONE
MATTHEW 25:31–40

"When the Son of Man comes in his glory, and all the angels with him, he will sit on his throne in heavenly glory. All the nations will be gathered before him, and he will separate the people one from another as a shepherd separates the sheep from the goats. He will put the sheep on his right and the goats on his left.

"Then the King will say to those on his right, 'Come, you who are blessed by my Father; take your inheritance, the kingdom prepared for you since the creation of the world. For I was hungry and you gave me something to eat, I was thirsty and you gave me something to drink, I was a stranger and you invited me in, I needed clothes and you clothed me, I was sick and you looked after me, I was in prison and you came to visit me.'

"Then the righteous will answer him, 'Lord, when did we see you hungry and feed you, or thirsty and give you something to drink? When did we see you a stranger and invite you in, or needing clothes and clothe you? When did we see you sick or in prison and go to visit you?'

"The King will reply, 'I tell you the truth, whatever you did for one of the least of these brothers of mine, you did for me.' "

"He's Going to Arrive at Noon Today!"

What are the entrance requirements for that place where you so long to be? What is the price of admission? Who provides access? Who opens the doors?

The doors of El Museo del Prado open at nine o'clock every morning except Monday. At eight-thirty on a Wednesday morning, I already was waiting at the main entrance, on the north side of the neoclassical building in the middle of Madrid.

For years it had been my dream to visit this place, which has the reputation of being one of the finest art museums in all the world. Inside, in addition to wondrous works from recognized masters of Western art, is the greatest collection of Spanish art in the entire world: El Greco, Ribalta, Ribera, Zurbaran, Velázquez, Murillo, Goya—all of them are represented here. In particular, there's a painting I've known since elementary school: *Las Meninas,* The Ladies in Waiting—the 1656 masterpiece by Diego Velázquez.

"This is the greatest work in the Prado," the museum's guidebook boasts, "and in Spanish painting as a whole, one of the most superb artistic achievements ever created, and the most valuable single piece of art in the museum."[1]

Way back in the third grade, for an art contest that my teacher insisted I enter, I had memorized the name of this picture, the artist and his country, and the date of the painting's creation. I had never forgotten *Las Meninas.* By the time I arrived in Madrid, I knew exactly where the picture was hanging: in gallery number 12, across the corridor from the ceremonial central entrance to the museum. I couldn't wait to get in.

The map of the museum directed visitors on a pathway to the left of gallery number 12, across the sprawling back expanse of the huge building to visit a series of smaller galleries, then up a far staircase to the second floor. When I entered the museum, I followed that pathway through those galleries and the vast, stunning Goya collection, then down again to the front corridor, ending at last in front of the Velázquez gallery.

I arrived at gallery number 12 at about 11:45, almost three hours after I entered the museum. *The best is yet to come!* I thought. "My painting" was just inside those closed doors—those closed doors that I suddenly realized had a wide red ribbon stretched across them, barring entrance. A sign, written in several languages, hung from the ribbon: "Closed for remodeling."

I peered frantically through the small vertical crack between the locked doors. I knocked, timidly at first and then with more conviction. I thought about trying to break in or at least attempting to bribe one of the guards. But even as I thought about it, I knew my attempts would fail, and, believing I never again would be this close, I began the bitter process of trying to resign myself to the idea that I'd never be in the presence of the great painting I so wanted to see.

Across the corridor and a little to the right, I stumbled into a small gift shop and wandered over to the wall where the museum's collection had been reduced to postcards. There it was, *Las Meninas,* the painting above all paintings I had come all this way to see. I took the postcard to the counter, held it up, and, hoping the cashier could understand a little English, I addressed her slowly and loudly, as American visitors to other countries so often do. "I don't suppose there is any way I can get in to see this painting," I said, trying to sound as pitiful as possible.

"I'm terribly sorry," she replied in perfect Oxford English. "The Velázquez gallery has been closed for several months now."

Then, suddenly, she gasped. "Oh, today is the day!" she almost shouted. "The president of Spain is scheduled to come to the Prado to reopen the gallery. And—" Here she paused and looked at her watch. "And he's going to arrive at noon today," she exclaimed, almost out of breath, "in just about five minutes!"

Almost before the words had escaped her lips, the corridor began to buzz. Guards opened the huge ceremonial front doors of the museum. People who knew of the president's imminent arrival jostled into place. Security people positioned themselves for protection. And above all, the curious ones, wondering about all the commotion, clamored for an unobstructed view.

It was true! At exactly twelve o'clock, three big, black limousines pulled up in front of the museum. A brass band began to play the Spanish equivalent to "Hail to the Chief." And then, there he was, smiling, waving, and greeting people he recognized. There was much applause, scores of flash pictures, the sudden appearance of a huge pair of scissors, and the wide, red ribbon was sundered in two. The gallery doors flew open, the dignitaries walked behind the president into gallery number 12—and the doors were shut behind them!

I held my breath. I could hear muffled conversation, polite applause, and scattered *oohs* and *aahs*. Then, just as suddenly as the doors had been shut behind the president, they opened again. He walked out, crossed the corridor, and descended the long stairway to his waiting limousine. It seemed everyone in the museum followed the president across the hallway and out the entrance to stand and watch as he got into his car and was driven away.

Everyone, that is, except me!

Gallery number 12 was open. No one was inside. And *Las Meninas* was hanging over there on the far wall. I walked in, crossed the gallery, and for a few precious minutes, stood alone in front of the great painting, reveling that I was at last where I had so longed to be.

Later that evening, back in my hotel room, I realized what had happened. I had experienced a moment of grace. What I couldn't accomplish on my own, the president of Spain had done for me. I couldn't get into gallery number 12. Only the president could open the doors and get me in.

---

1. Alicia Quintans, *Guide, Prado Museum* (Madrid, Spain: Aldeasa, 1994), 44.

Diego Velásquez, *Las Meninas* (The Ladies in Waiting)
To view this painting in color, go to www.pacificpress.com/chosenbygrace.

Chapter One
Saved by the Everlasting Gospel

What are you going to be doing ten million years from today? What do you imagine for that place that "no eye has seen, no ear has heard, no mind has conceived" (1 Corinthians 2:9)? How are you going to get there?

As much as we love our home in southern California, there is a considerable contrast between where Karen and I have been living for the past twenty years and where we're going to spend eternity. Sometimes the traffic on the freeways here is so congested that the usual one-hour trip to Los Angeles takes almost three hours; in our eternal home, the redeemed will fly—they will "soar on wings like eagles" (Isaiah 40:31)! Here, there are recurring potholes on Sierra Vista Avenue; in the Holy City, the streets are paved with gold (Revelation 21:21). Here, we struggle to keep the weeds from taking over our front yard; in the earth made new,

"Instead of the thorn bush will grow
the pine tree,
and instead of briers the myrtle
will grow.
This will be for the LORD's renown,
for an everlasting sign,
which will not be destroyed"
(Isaiah 55:13).

"The LORD will surely comfort Zion
and will look with compassion on
all her ruins;
he will make her deserts like Eden,
her wastelands like the garden of
the LORD.
Joy and gladness will be found in her,
thanksgiving and the sound of
singing" (Isaiah 51:3).

"Behold, I will create
new heavens and a new earth.
The former things will not be remembered,
nor will they come to mind"
(Isaiah 65:17).

There are other, more consequential things I'm not going to miss in heaven. I've spent too many hours in hospitals visiting dear friends desperately fighting life-threatening diseases. I've jumped in the back of an ambulance to hold the hand of a friend who had just been pulled from the wreckage of an accident in which her daughter had been killed. I've known people who have died in military battles and terrorist attacks and genocidal insurrections. I've preached too many funeral sermons. I've counseled too many couples through the bitter disintegration of their once cherished marriages.

Someday that's all going to change.

> The ransomed of the LORD will
> return.
> They will enter Zion with singing;
> everlasting joy will crown
> their heads.
> Gladness and joy will overtake
> them,
> and sorrow and sighing will
> flee away (Isaiah 35:10).

That's where I'm going to be ten million years from now!

The Bible assures us of our eternal home and asks us to be confident. We are chosen by grace, adopted, redeemed, included, marked in Him with a seal, "the promised Holy Spirit, who is a deposit *guaranteeing* our inheritance" (Ephesians 1:1–14).* In Jesus "we *have* redemption through his blood, the forgiveness of sins, in accordance with the riches of God's grace" (1:7). "God has given us eternal life, and this life is in his Son. *He who has the Son has life*" (1 John 5:11, 12). We are to "stand firm in all the will of God, mature and fully assured" (Colossians 4:12). "Let us draw near to God with a sincere heart in full assurance of faith, having our hearts sprinkled to cleanse us from a guilty conscience and having our bodies washed with pure water. Let us hold unswervingly to the hope we profess, *for he who prom-*

> " 'See, your Savior comes!
> See, his reward is with him,
> and his recompense
> accompanies him.'
> They will be called the Holy People,
> the Redeemed of the LORD;
> and you will be called Sought After,
> the City No Longer Deserted"
> (Isaiah 62:11, 12).

"He will wipe every tear from their eyes. There will be no more death or mourning or crying or pain, for the old order of things has passed away" (Revelation 21:4).

---

*Unless otherwise noted, all emphasis in quotations from Scripture in this book has been added.

ised is faithful" (Hebrews 10:22, 23).

This biblical assurance of salvation, however, actually can be unsettling to people who have grown up in churches that have spoken less of God's role in our salvation and more about our part in the experience. Everywhere I preach, people approach me to voice their caution. Many of these careful folk are fearful that grace is just a capricious deception that leads ultimately to a disregard of God's perfect law and a laxness in our Christian journey. This worry also shadowed Jude, the brother of James, who grappled with "godless men, who change the grace of our God into a license for immorality and deny Jesus Christ our only Sovereign and Lord" (Jude 4).

Is there, in fact, something intrinsically perilous in the Bible's assurance of salvation? Does the promise of eternal life predispose us to hold tenaciously to a disadvantageous, "once saved, always saved no matter what we do" attitude? To address this apprehension, let's examine the Bible's five cardinal assertions about how salvation operates: there is an end; there is a judgment; there is a standard in the judgment; that standard condemns us all; and God has established a way to save us.

THERE IS AN END

First of all, the Bible insists that this present world will end.

The oppressor will come to an
    end,
        and destruction will cease;
        the aggressor will vanish from
            the land.
In love a throne will be estab-
    lished (Isaiah 1:4, 5).

"I will return" (Zechariah 8:3).

"This same Jesus . . . will come back"
    (Acts 1:11).

"The trumpet will sound, the dead will be raised imperishable, and we will be changed" (1 Corinthians 15:52).

"The Lord himself will come down from heaven, with a loud command, with the voice of the archangel and with the trumpet call of God, and the dead in Christ will rise first. After that, we who are still alive and are left will be caught up together with them in the clouds to meet the Lord in the air. And so we will be with the Lord forever. Therefore encourage each other with these words" (1 Thessalonians 4:16–18).

"I am coming soon" (Revelation 22:20).

"The God of heaven will set up a kingdom that will never be destroyed, nor will it be left to another people. It will crush all those kingdoms and bring them to an end, but it will itself endure forever" (Daniel 2:44). "This gospel of the kingdom will be preached in the whole world as a testimony to all nations, and then the end will come" (Matthew 24:14).

No matter how we refer to that day—the Second Coming, the end of the age, the day of the Lord—the Bible's position is resolute: There will be an end! "Our God shall come, and shall not keep silence" (Psalm 50:3, KJV). "I will come back" (John 14:1–3).

On that long-anticipated day, heralded by trumpet blasts and thunder and lightning, we will hear two distinct voices speaking people's reactions to Jesus' return. One voice welcomes the end of this world's history, rejoices at the return of the Savior, and proclaims with confidence,

"Surely this is our God;
we trusted in him, and he saved us.
This is the Lord, we trusted in him;
let us rejoice and be glad in his salvation" (Isaiah 25:9).

"Hallelujah!
For our Lord God Almighty reigns.
Let us rejoice and be glad and give him glory!
For the wedding of the Lamb has come" (Revelation 19:6, 7).

The second voice, just as loud and just as distinct, is a fearful cry. "Listen!" the prophet Zephaniah summons us.

"The cry on the day of the Lord will be bitter,
the shouting of the warrior there.
That day will be a day of wrath,
a day of distress and anguish,
a day of trouble and ruin,
a day of darkness and gloom"
(Zephaniah 1:14, 15).

"Wail, for the day of the Lord is near," Isaiah warns (Isaiah 13:4–6). Ezekiel paints that day as a day of doom (Ezekiel 30:3). Joel calls it "dreadful" (Joel 2:11). Amos describes it as a day of darkness "without a ray of brightness" (Amos 5:20). Jesus says that people will mourn (Matthew 24:30). John hears people saying to the rocks and mountains, "Fall on us and hide us from the face of him who sits on the throne" (Revelation 6:16).

Two voices: one is full of confidence, trust, joy, and gladness. The other is fearful, a mournful wail, a bitter, stressed, and gloomy cry.

What makes the difference?

Here's the answer: The confident group has done their crying earlier. "They cried out to the LORD in their trouble, / and he delivered them from their distress" (Psalm 107:6). They had "wandered in desert wastelands" (107:4). They had been hungry and thirsty (107:5). They had "sat in darkness and the deepest gloom" (107:10). "They had rebelled against the words of God and despised the counsel of the Most High" (107:11, 17). Their courage had failed (107:26). They "reeled and staggered like drunken men; / they were at their wits' end" (107:27). They had been humbled (107:39).

And in those earlier, humbling times of trouble, as they struggled with their commitment, as they grappled with the temptation to be confident in themselves rather than in God, as they wrestled with despair, they discovered God's saving power. *He* breaks away our chains (107:14). *He* heals and rescues us (107:20). *He* stills our storms to a calming whisper (107:29, 30). *He* turns parched ground into flowing springs (107:35).

Now the confident ones "see and rejoice" (107:42) and express their gratitude to God "for his unfailing love" (107:8, 15, 21, 31).

> Give thanks to the Lord, for He is
>   good!
> For His mercy endures forever.
> Let the redeemed of the Lord say
>   so (107:1, 2, NKJV).

"Whoever is wise, let him heed these things / and consider the great love of the LORD" (107:43).

First of all, the Bible assures us that there is an end.

THERE IS A JUDGMENT

Second, the Bible makes it clear that there is a judgment.

"The LORD will bring charges against the nations. / He will bring judgment on all mankind" (Jeremiah 25:31). "He has set a day when he will judge the world," Paul preached in Athens (Acts 17:31). "We will all stand before God's judgment seat" (Romans 14:10).

Many of us grew up dreading the Judgment Day, hoping it wouldn't happen anytime soon, and pretending that if we didn't think too much about it, maybe the subject would just go away. Someone drew the connecting lines for us, or we intuitively connected by ourselves the public end-time judgment with a long list of private, personal transgressions, and the conviction grew that one day everyone in the world would know exactly how rebellious we really had been. "The judgment was set, and the books were opened" (Daniel 7:10). "Men will have to give account on the day of judgment for every careless word they have spoken" (Matthew 12:36). "God will judge men's secrets," Paul added ominously (Romans 2:16).

"The LORD will judge the ends of the earth" (1 Samuel 2:10).

"We must all appear before the judgment seat of Christ" (2 Corinthians 5:10).

"God will bring every deed into judgment,
including every hidden thing,
whether it is good or evil" (Ecclesiastes 12:14).

"The books were opened: and another book was opened, which is the book of life: and the dead were judged out of those things which were written in the books" (Revelation 20:12, KJV).

Yet the Bible presents a startling picture of this final judgment, exactly as it presents the picture of the end of time. While the judgment is feared by the wicked, by evildoers, by those who are afraid to look into the face of the righteous Judge, it isn't feared at all by those who trust God! For people whose confidence is in the Lord and whose life is in His hands, the judgment holds no dread, no fear, and no worries. "Those who trust in the LORD are like Mount Zion, / which cannot be shaken" (Psalm 125:1).

We are encouraged *to look forward to* the time of judgment, to trust in the righteous decisions of an all-knowing God whose love, goodness, faithfulness, and righteousness endure forever (1 Chronicles 16:34; Psalms 100:5; 112:3; 117:2).

Let the heavens rejoice, let the
earth be glad;
let the sea resound, and all that
is in it;
let the fields be jubilant, and
everything in them.
Then all the trees of the forest will
sing for joy;
they will sing before the
LORD, for he comes,
he comes to judge the earth.

He will judge the world in righteousness
  and the peoples in his truth
    (Psalm 96:11–13).

Let the rivers clap their hands,
  let the mountains sing together for joy;
let them sing before the LORD,
  for he comes to judge the earth.
He will judge the world in righteousness
  and the peoples with equity
    (Psalm 98:8, 9).

"You will keep in perfect peace
  him whose mind is steadfast,
  because he trusts in you.
Trust in the LORD forever,
  for the LORD, the LORD, is the
    Rock eternal" (Isaiah 26:3, 4).

"We know and rely on the love God has for us.

"God is love. Whoever lives in love lives in God, and God in him. In this way, love is made complete among us so that we will have confidence on the day of judgment, because in this world we are like him. There is no fear in love. But perfect love drives out fear, because fear has to do with punishment" (1 John 4:16–18).

THERE IS A STANDARD IN THE JUDGMENT

How will we stand in this final judgment? What will determine the verdict?

When the rich, eager, young ruler runs up to Jesus and asks, "What must I do to get eternal life?" Jesus answers him with a straightforward yet comprehensive reply. "If you would enter life," Jesus says, "obey the commandments" (Matthew 19:16–26; Mark 10:17–27; Luke 18:18–27). Jesus isn't talking about just an *occasional* obedience. He isn't suggesting that *every now and then* we ought to add another check mark to our list of obeyed commands. He isn't recommending that we keep most of the commandments most of the time. He's referring to an all-embracing, 100-percent, all-our-life obedience. "Whoever keeps the whole law and yet stumbles at just one point is guilty of breaking all of it" (James 2:10). The standard Jesus holds up to the young man is *perfect obedience* (Matthew 19:21); obeying all of God's law all of the time. And to be sure that we see the high standard, Jesus adds *perfect motivation* to the qualification.

So, here's the formula: Perfect obedience to the perfect law of God plus perfect motivation (always doing the right thing for the right reason) equals perfect righteousness. "Judgment will again be

"Rise up, O Judge of the earth; / pay back to the proud what they deserve" (Psalm 94:2).

"Repay them for their deeds
and for their evil work;
repay them for what their hands have done
and bring back upon them what
they deserve" (Psalm 28:4).

"Reward each person / according to what he has done" (Psalm 62:12).

"Pay them back . . . / for what their hands have done" (Lamentations 3:64).

"The dead were judged according to what they had done as recorded in the books. . . . Each person was judged according to what he had done" (Revelation 20:12, 13).

founded on righteousness" (Psalm 94:15). Perfect righteousness is what it takes to earn—"to get"—eternal life.

The discourse that takes place between those who are confident in the biblical assurance of salvation and those who are worried about where that assurance might lead often grinds to a halt at this point. The worried side prefers to end the story of the rich, young ruler with the qualification, "If you would enter life, obey the commandments." There it is, they argue, simple and plain, easy enough for all of us to understand: "obey the command-

ments." And then, so that we don't miss the point they believe Jesus is making, preachers from this side of the discussion quote Paul's similar condition-setting admonition: "It is not those who hear the law who are righteous in God's sight, but it is those who obey the law who will be declared righteous" (Romans 2:13).

The Old Testament lays the foundation for the doctrine Jesus sets forth to the rich, young ruler. Jeremiah tells us that God warns, "I will repay them according to their deeds and the work of their hands" (Jeremiah 25:14). And Hosea says that God "will punish Jacob according to his ways / and repay him according to his deeds" (Hosea 12:2).

Quoting the Psalms, Paul adds to the discussion. "God 'will give to each person according to what he has done.' To those who by persistence in doing good seek glory, honor and immortality, he will give eternal life. But for those who are self-seeking and who reject the truth and follow evil, there will be wrath and anger" (Romans 2:6, 7). The book of Revelation repeats the doctrine: "I will repay each of you according to your deeds" (Revelation 2:23).

There is an end. There is a judgment. There is a standard: perfect righteousness.

THAT STANDARD CONDEMNS US ALL

If the standard is perfect righteousness, who then will be saved?

When the rich ruler hears Jesus state the qualification for eternal life, he realizes that both his obedience and his motivation have been *imperfect* and is shocked. "That was the last thing the young man expected to hear" (Matthew 19:22, *The Message*). Crestfallen, he walks away.

Joining the young man in his dismay, the disciples are so stunned by Jesus' answer—so "greatly astonished" Matthew tells us—that they can only blurt out, "Who then can be saved?" (19:25).

Jesus replies, "With people this is impossible" (19:26, NASB).

Jesus wasn't introducing a new doctrine here. The formula was in play long before people began voicing the questions, "Who can endure the day of his coming?" and "Who can stand when he appears?" (Malachi 3:2; Nahum 1:6).

The Bible's answer to these questions is as clear as it possibly can be. On the basis of perfect righteousness, Paul writes,

there is no one righteous, not
     even one.
There is no one who
     understands,
no one who seeks God.

All have turned away,
     they have together become
          worthless;
there is no one who does good,
     not even one (Romans 3:10–
     12).

How many will be judged righteous by their obedience, their good works, or their overcoming? "By observing the law *no one* will be justified" (Galatians 2:16). "*All* have sinned and fall short of the glory of God" (Romans 3:23). Paul answers his own argument that only those who obey the law will be declared righteous (Romans 2:13) by insisting that judged against this perfect standard "*no one* will be declared righteous in his sight by observing the law" (3:20).

The ancient serpent called the devil or Satan "leads *the whole world* astray" (Revelation 12:9). "*All* the inhabitants of the earth" (13:8), "*everyone,* small and great, rich and poor, free and slave" (13:16), "*all* the nations" are led astray (18:23). All of us. Everyone. Even those who worship God. Even end-time people. Even the remnant. We've all fallen short. There are no exceptions.

So, there is an end. There is a judgment. There is a standard: perfect righteousness. And that standard condemns us all.

> "The sinful mind is hostile to God. It does not submit to God's will, nor can it do so" (Romans 8:7).
>
> "Do not bring your servant into judgment, / for *no one* living is righteous before you" (Psalm 143:2).
>
> "We have sinned and done wrong. We have been wicked and have rebelled; we have turned away from your commands and laws. We have not listened to your servants the prophets, who spoke in your name to our kings, our princes and our fathers, and to all the people of the land.
>   "Lord, you are righteous, but this day we are covered with shame—the men of Judah and people of Jerusalem and all Israel, both near and far, in all the countries where you have scattered us because of our unfaithfulness to you. O Lord, we and our kings, our princes and our fathers are covered with shame because we have sinned against you. . . . We have not obeyed the Lord our God or kept the laws he gave us through his servants the prophets. *All* Israel has transgressed your law and turned away, refusing to obey you" (Daniel 9:5–11).
>
> "Here we are before you in our guilt, though because of it *not one of us* can stand in your presence" (Ezra 9:15).

GOD HAS ESTABLISHED A WAY TO SAVE US

Mercifully, that's not the end of the story. To understand why, we have to go back to the beginning of the story.

At a watershed moment in eternal prehistoric time, before the foundation of this world had been laid or earth's dimensions had been marked off, the omniscient Godhead held a salvation council. "While the morning stars sang together and all the angels shouted for joy," was made a decision and was given a gift. Gazing with unfaltering vision into a chronicle that was yet to be written, They were confronted by an ultimate, painful reality. They knew that in spite of the enormous outpouring of Their love and notwithstanding Their constant nurturing presence, humans one day would choose darkness over light (John 3:19). And with that choice would come a *stumbling* (11:9, 10), a falling away, until people would not only misunderstand the light (1:5), they would actually come to love the darkness rather than the light (3:19).

The God in whom "there is no darkness at all" (1 John 1:5) was faced with three distinct alternatives:

1. The Godhead could simply abandon Their plans for the creation of planet Earth. They could walk away and reserve Their creating for some other stage where Their endeavors would be appreciated. "You are worthy, our Lord and God,"

someone else would have to sing,

> to receive glory and honor and
> power,
> for you created all things,
>> and by your will they were cre-
>> ated and have their being
>> (Revelation 4:11).

2. The Godhead could continue with Their creation plans and *then* walk away from earth, relinquishing any responsibility for Their fallen creatures. They could leave humanity confused (Psalm 82:5) and in total darkness, without any hope for anything other than more darkness, "thrown outside, into the darkness, where there will be weeping and gnashing of teeth" (Matthew 8:12). "Justice is far from us," the humans would cry, "and righteousness does not reach us. / We look for light, but all is darkness; for brightness, but we walk in deep shadows" (Isaiah 59:9).

3. Or the Godhead could continue with Their plans to create this world knowing what would happen and what the consequences of the stumbling would mean. They would have to do for us that which it is impossible for us to do for ourselves. They would have to step into human history in a way They had never done before at any other place in the galaxies. And by fully demonstrating Their love to sinful human beings (Romans 5:8), the Godhead would call those people out of darkness into Their wonderful light (1 Peter 2:9).

In that moment, the Member of the Godhead we call by His human name, Jesus, intentionally, purposefully chose to become "the Lamb that was slain from the creation of the world" (Revelation 13:8). "Before the creation of the world" (Ephesians 1:4), He chose to save us eternally.

For the people of our planet, the act of Creation was an act of grace.

God's determination to establish a relationship of grace with humanity grounds our faith, a faith "resting on the hope of eternal life, which God, who does not lie, promised before the beginning of time" (Titus 1:2). "Not because of anything we have done but because of his own purpose and grace. This grace was given us in Christ Jesus before the beginning of time" (2 Timothy 1:9). Now, "we who have fled to take hold of the hope offered to us may be greatly encouraged. We have this hope as an anchor for the soul, firm and secure" (Hebrews 6:18, 19).

Here is where the story of the rich, young ruler comes to its rightful conclusion. Who then can be saved? With people it is impossible, Jesus explains, "but with God all things are possible" (Matthew 19:26).

Once saved?

Absolutely.

Before the world was created, our names were written in the Lamb's book of life.

Before any human being could merit eternity, the promise of heaven was ours.

Before all of us had sinned and forfeited the ability to contribute to our salvation, we were already saved.

Before the "only begotten Son" died on the cross, God already loved us (John 3:16; Romans 5:6–8).

Before any of us felt we had to plead and beg for forgiveness, we were already forgiven.

Before you and I were born, we were saved.

Always saved?

It can be that way.

But, as difficult as this is to believe, the same Bible that assures us that our salvation is sure by grace alone also reports the tragic statistic that millions of human beings, a host as numerous as the sand on

the seashore (Revelation 20:8), will reject the salvation that has been theirs since before the creation of the world. They will demand that their names be stricken from the Lamb's book of life. They will choose to fight the Lamb to the bitter end, preferring to conclude their existence in "outer darkness" (Matthew 22:13).

We can escape "the corruption of the world by knowing our Lord and Savior Jesus Christ." We can know "the way of righteousness." And we can turn our backs on it (2 Peter 2:20, 21). We have been saved from the beginning. We are predestined for eternal life (Ephesians 1:4–6). But that destiny is never forced on us once and for all. If we prefer, we can say No to grace.

On the other hand, God's end-time people, assured, encouraged, anchored, and secure, say Yes.

"Come, you who are blessed by my Father," Jesus invites us. "Take your inheritance, the kingdom prepared for you since the creation of the world" (Matthew 25:34).

With great joy, we accept the invitation.

"Can we repair our broken relationship with God? Can we perform works to appease God? No, for nothing we can ever do removes the guilt of our past sins, and nothing we do is free from the stain of sinful motives and corruption. In short, we cannot save ourselves and God must therefore save us. Ephesians 2:4 explains this, first drawing out the true extent of our problem in sin but then pointing to our only hope: 'God, being rich in mercy.' Our hope of salvation, our pathway to peace, is the grace of God, who is rich in mercy. . . .

"Grace is often defined as God's unmerited favor. That is true, but it does not go far enough. Grace is God's favor to us when we have merited the opposite. We have earned his hatred and wrath and condemnation. And yet he causes us to be forgiven and made his precious children. He brings us into his household and lavishes us with every good thing. He gives that which is most precious to himself—his only Son."

—Richard Phillips, *Chosen in Christ*

"The sad fact is that the church, both now and at far too many times in its history, has found it easier to act as if it were selling the sugar of moral and spiritual achievement rather than the salt of Jesus' passion and death. It will preach salvation for the successfully well-behaved, redemption for the triumphantly correct in doctrine, and pie in the sky for the winners who think they can walk into the final judgment and flash their passing report cards at Jesus. But every last bit of that is now and ever shall be pure baloney because: (a) nobody will ever have that kind of sugar to sweeten the last deal with, and (b) Jesus is going to present us all to the Father in the power of *his* resurrection and not at all in the power of our own totally inadequate records, either good or bad. . . . It is precisely our sins, and not our goodnesses, that most commend us to the grace of God."

—Robert Farrar Capon, *The Parables of Grace*

Vision Number Two
Ezra 9:6–15

"O my God, I am too ashamed and disgraced to lift up my face to you, my God, because our sins are higher than our heads and our guilt has reached to the heavens. From the days of our forefathers until now, our guilt has been great. Because of our sins, we and our kings and our priests have been subjected to the sword and captivity, to pillage and humiliation at the hand of foreign kings, as it is today.

"But now, for a brief moment, the LORD our God has been gracious in leaving us a remnant and giving us a firm place in his sanctuary, and so our God gives light to our eyes and a little relief in our bondage. Though we are slaves, our God has not deserted us in our bondage. He has shown us kindness in the sight of the kings of Persia: He has granted us new life to rebuild the house of our God and repair its ruins, and he has given us a wall of protection in Judah and Jerusalem.

"But now, O our God, what can we say after this? For we have disregarded the commands you gave through your servants the prophets. . . .

"What has happened to us is a result of our evil deeds and our great guilt, and yet, our God, you have punished us less than our sins have deserved and have given us a remnant like this. Shall we again break your commands? . . .
Would you not be angry enough with us to destroy us, leaving us
no remnant or survivor? O LORD, God of Israel, you are
righteous! We are left this day as a remnant. Here we are
before you in our guilt, though because of it not one
of us can stand in your presence."

INTRODUCING CHAPTER TWO
GROUNDED IN BIBLICAL REALITIES

Might the history of art teach us anything about how to study the Bible? Can we discover principles that establish a better way to understand familiar passages or a more accurate way to ground biblical characters in the realities of the Bible story?

L ook carefully at an Egyptian painting from about 2000 B.C. Notice the feet. What's missing?

Now observe a fresco from the royal palace of Knossos on Crete, painted five hundred years later. Look at the feet of the people. Notice anything strange?

A pattern begins to emerge. Something is striking by its absence. On fifth-century B.C. Greek vases. On wall paintings in Roman catacombs from the first century after Christ. On those magnificent sixth-century mosaics from Ravenna. On the Bayeux Tapestry from the end of the eleventh century. On the fourteenth-century masterpieces of Cimabue, Duccio, Simone Martini, and even Giotto. Are you looking at the feet? Do you see what's not there?

From the time of ancient Egypt to the Middle Ages, artists painted people as if they were hovering just a few inches above the ground or standing on their tiptoes. There are no cast shadows. No matter how colorful the paintings are, or how carefully drawn are the figures, or how striking the backgrounds, the feet are just not quite right—dangling sometimes, not attaching the people to the landscape, not *grounded*.

Until a young man named Masaccio. The name his mother gave him at his birth was Tommaso di Ser Giovanni di Mone Cassai. We know him by a nickname, "Big, hulky, rough"—*Masaccio*. He was born near Florence, Italy, on December 21, 1401. He died before his twenty-seventh birthday. In his short career as an artist, Masaccio completed only a handful of major projects. Yet, Botticelli admired his works; Leonardo paid him tribute; Michelangelo copied him; and Raphael found him to be an inspiration. Vasari, the early biographer of the great artists, tells us that he was chiefly responsible for the excellence of the Florentine painters. Other writers call him a revolutionary figure, and "arguably the most influential painter who ever lived."

If you question that accolade, just look at the feet of the people in his paintings. Masaccio's people are grounded! Adam and Eve stumble forward, overcome with uncontrollable grief—their feet firmly planted on the soil *outside* the Garden of Eden. The adoring Magi come to stand before the Christ Child, who seems to be the source of the light that throws the Magis' shadows backward, solidly positioning their feet on Bethlehem's ground. In an animated conversation about taxation, the disciples surround Jesus, and their feet cast shadows to the left, the light obviously coming from a source high up and to the right. Peter walks by three men who need healing, and as he passes, his shadow moves over them and heals them, and they begin to rise.

Masaccio's shadows impart a new significance to the human figure. Suddenly, the people being painted have a fresh appearance, a revived dimension. The shadows help us get acquainted with diverse individual personalities who we used to know only as a group—like Peter and John, who before we saw only as disciples. Masaccio makes his people believable. Before him, the subjects in paintings were plausible—relatively accurate representations of people. But somehow they weren't real. Now we see the characters—even the biblical characters of Masaccio's art—as nonfictitious and, perhaps even more importantly, as people just like us. "Everything done before him," Giorgio Vasari reflects, "can be described as artificial, whereas he produced work that is living, realistic, and natural."

Furthermore, while Masaccio's shadows ground the techniques of depiction, they

Masaccio (Tommaso di Ser Giovanni di Mone Cassai), *Tribute Money*
To view this painting in color, go to www.pacificpress.com/chosenbygrace.

don't contradict the realities he paints. The subjects of his paintings—Adam and Eve, the Magi, Jesus and His disciples—*did* cast shadows! Their feet *did* make contact with the ground! Masaccio simply insists that painters follow nature as closely as possible, believing that art is more convincing when it more carefully portrays the original actualities.

But Masaccio wasn't satisfied with his early successes. In order to progress in his art, he traveled to Rome to study other great artists and accept commissions that enabled him to work out what he was learning. In these projects, his skill became renowned. The commissions multiplied—and with them the envy of lesser artists. Masaccio's sudden death at so early an age was so unexpected that the whispers began to circulate that a jealous rival had poisoned him.

When news of his untimely death reached his Florentine friend Filippo Brunelleschi, the great architect reported that he was "plunged into grief." At Masaccio's funeral, one admiring mourner left these words: "In this one death there dies all painting's charm. With this sun's quenching, all the stars are quenched; beside this fall, alas, all beauty falls."

Masaccio approached art the way Christians approach the study of biblical topics.

Our study must be grounded in the realities of the Bible. Our understandings must be scriptural. With an open, receptive heart we stand in the light that streams from the pages of the Bible—ever new and fresh, ever contemporary and relevant—and in that light we daily discover pristine depths of spiritual meaning that animate and shape our lives and take away the artificiality.

It is a risky strategy, this grounding our beliefs in the Bible, but one of rich reward. It may mean that we look at things a little differently than we've looked at them before. But after all, had Masaccio only painted people the way the great Giotto had painted them, we'd all still be standing on our tiptoes.[1]

---

1. See Giorgio Vasari, *The Lives of the Artists* (Oxford: Oxford University Press, translation published 1991), 101–109. Unless otherwise noted, quotations referring to Masaccio and his paintings are from this publication.

CHAPTER TWO
CHOSEN BY GRACE

*What do the Bible's stories about remnant people teach us about God?
How do these stories ground us in the gospel? How do they help us
respond when God gives us a remnant message?*

I
s the biblical doctrine of the end-time remnant about you and me? Or is it about God?

Is it about our determined attempts to obey and overcome and somehow become "safe to save"? Or is it about God's active, zealous commitment to give us the gift of salvation?

Is the doctrine about how faithful and loyal we are or should be? Or is the proper focus on God's persistent love, His unfailing goodness, and His enduring grace?

Does the Bible teach that the remnant is a group of people who live at the end of earth's history, who have tried so hard to be so good that God is compelled to reward them with eternal life? Or is the Bible's instruction on the remnant more about God, who over and over again has singled out a small group of ordinary people and given them an extraordinary mission—to draw attention to His everlasting love and long-suffering faithfulness?[1]

I have been among those Adventists who have been troubled about the remnant doctrine. As I had so often heard it explained and as I had taught it for so many years, it somehow came across as arrogant and exclusionary. Further, and even more importantly, it was, I realized, poorly grounded in what the Bible actually teaches.

One Sabbath not too long ago, after I preached a sermon at a distant camp meeting, a woman approached me and declared that she had decided that week to stop being a Seventh-day Adventist. "I don't believe in the remnant doctrine anymore," she explained. "I can't belong to a church that thinks that way."

I understood. The temptation also had assailed me and many of my Adventist friends. I realized that I needed to study the entire end-time scenario more seriously than I ever had before. These chapters are a result of that study.

Much to my surprise, I discovered that what the Bible teaches us about "remnancy" is absolutely beautiful and remarkably winsome! It is Christ-centered and grace-oriented. It inspires grateful worship, builds community, and motivates humble service. It is never arrogant, never prescribed, never exclusive, never self-serving.

THE EARLIEST REMNANT PEOPLE

The Bible's stunning story of God's relationship with remnant people begins at the beginning, not the end—in the book of Genesis, not the book of Revelation.[2]

Eight people kneel around an altar on Mount Ararat and listen to the promise God gives them from beyond a rainbow (Genesis 8:20, 21; 9:12–17). Before the Deluge, these people had looked deeply into the eyes of God and found grace (6:8). They are survivors because God is a gracious Savior, not because they are particularly savable, as the end of chapter 9 quickly tells us. Now they are the only ones left from the antediluvian world.

The remaining few from a once populous planet. The leftovers. The remnant.

> "If the LORD had not been on our
>   side—
>   let Israel say . . .
> the flood would have engulfed us,
>   the torrent would have swept
>   over us,
> the raging waters would have swept us
>   away" (Psalm 124:1–5).
>
> "God Almighty appeared to me . . . in the land of Canaan, and there he blessed me and said to me, "I am going to make you fruitful and will increase your numbers. I will make you a community of peoples, and I will give this land as an everlasting possession to your descendants after you" (Genesis 48:3, 4).
>
> "I, the LORD have called you
>   in righteousness,
>   I will take hold of your hand.
> I will keep you and will make you
>   to be a covenant for the people"
>   (Isaiah 42:6).

Later in Genesis, another remnant appears. Eleven brothers bow humbly before "the governor of the land" (Genesis 42:6). They have been accused of stealing and lying to the authorities (chapter 44). They are terrified and stressed (45:3–5), but not because of the accusation. The governor has just revealed that he is their long-lost brother, the one they wanted to kill, the one they sold into slavery, the one they lied about to their father. Graciously, Joseph forgives them and credits the big picture to God's leading. "God sent me ahead of you," he says, "to save your lives by a great deliverance" (45:7). To rescue them. To preserve them as a remnant.

Another group of people is also called a remnant. King Hezekiah is repentant and fearful for his life (2 Kings 18:14). Though he is the best of all the kings of Judah (18:3–5), Jerusalem is in immediate danger of falling to the sizable army of the Assyrians. "This is a day of distress and rebuke and disgrace," Hezekiah reflects to Isaiah, asking the prophet to pray for them (19:3, 4). Isaiah responds, "[The] people, drained of power, / are dismayed and put to shame." But "out of Jerusalem will come a remnant, / . . . a band of survivors" (19:26, 31).

We encounter yet another remnant. Jerusalem falls, this time to Nebuchadnezzar, king of the neo-Babylonian empire. Nebuchadnezzar hauls away

all the articles from the temple of God, both large and small, and the treasures of the LORD's temple and the treasures of the king and his officials. They set fire to God's temple and broke down the wall of Jerusalem; they burned all the palaces and destroyed everything of value there.

He carried into exile to Babylon the remnant, who escaped from the sword, and they became servants to him and his sons until the kingdom of Persia came to power (2 Chronicles 36:18–20).

The protective wall of the city is in ruins. The temple is destroyed. The palaces burned. Zedekiah, the king of Judah, is blinded and transported to Babylon in shackles. Only the very poor are left behind—people who own nothing. Nebuchadnezzar appoints Gedaliah to be governor in Judah (Jeremiah 39). The prophet Jeremiah is chained among the remnant, the survivors, the group being marched into exile. He is freed and permitted to remain "among the people who were left behind in the land," another remnant (40:1–6).

JEREMIAH IS INTRODUCED TO ANOTHER REMNANT

We meet a different remnant.

Shortly after the Babylonians leave, a group of Judah's army officers and soldiers and other Jews who had been scattered in the defeat return to Judah and travel to Mizpah to consult with the new governor. Gedaliah attempts to reassure them and promises to represent them before the Babylonians. "Settle down in the land," Gedaliah instructs, "harvest the wine, summer fruit and oil, and put them in your storage jars" (40:9, 10).

But among the refugees is a man named Ishmael who has his doubts about this Babylonian-appointed governor. Ishmael has gone to work for Baalis, king of the Ammonites, and Baalis wants Gedaliah killed. Ishmael accepts the assignment. At a banquet held by the governor, Ishmael and ten mercenaries carry out a successful assassination. Not content, the group also kills fellow Jews who are supporters of Gedaliah in Mizpah, and then, to try to conceal their deeds, they kill the Babylonian soldiers who are there (41:1–3). Undeterred, they go on a killing spree and then take captive another group, intending to sell them into slavery to the Ammonites. On the way out of Mizpah, a band of rescuers catches up with Ishmael and his soldiers and frees the captives. Ishmael and eight of his men escape (41:4–15).

Now the story takes a fascinating turn, one that deepens our understanding of the Bible doctrine of the remnant.

The rescuers of the captives, led by a man named Johanan, are afraid that Nebuchadnezzar will hear about Ishmael's assassination of Gedaliah and the Babylonian soldiers and will return to Judah and carry out wholesale retaliation on whoever is left in the city. So instead of returning to Mizpah, they turn south and head toward Egypt, to try to build a new life for themselves there and, in the process, hide from the Babylonians (41:16–18).

> "We do not make requests of you because we are righteous, but because of your great mercy. O Lord, listen! O Lord, forgive! O Lord, hear and act! For your sake, O my God, do not delay" (Daniel 9:18, 19).
>
> "You came near when I called you,
>   and you said, 'Do not fear.'
> O Lord, you took up my case;
>   you redeemed my life"
>   (Lamentations 3:57, 58).

On the way, the refugees stop at a village near Bethlehem where Jeremiah is now living. As soon as Johanan sees Jeremiah, he asks for the prophet's blessing on their venture. "Please hear our petition and pray to the LORD your God for this entire remnant," Johanan pleads. "For as you now see, though we were once many, now only a few are left. Pray that the

LORD your God will tell us where we should go and what we should do." And when you give us the answer, they add, "we will obey the LORD our God" no matter what He tells us to do (42:1–6).

So far this remnant group looks pretty good, doesn't it? They've rescued their friends. They've exercised some common-sense defensive maneuvers. They've gone to the prophet and asked for God's guidance. They've promised to be obedient. Perhaps this is what we've been looking for—remnant people who are committed to doing the right thing, remnant people we can use as a pattern for the behavior of an end-time remnant. But wait!

Jeremiah returns ten days later with a definite answer. "This is what the LORD . . . says," the prophet reports. " 'If you stay in this land, I will build you up and not tear you down. . . . Do not be afraid of the king of Babylon, whom you now fear. Do not be afraid of him, declares the LORD, for I am with you and will save you and deliver you from his hands. I will show you compassion so that he will have compassion on you and restore you to your land.' " Stay right here in this relationship to Me. Your future prosperity depends on your trusting My word.

However, if you disobey and determine to follow your own pathway, if you leave this relationship we have, if you try to save yourself from your enemy instead of letting Me save you, then let Me tell you what the consequences are going to be. "Hear the word of the LORD, O remnant of Judah. This is what the LORD Almighty, the God of Israel, says: 'If you are determined to go to Egypt and you do go to settle there, then the sword you fear will overtake you there, and the famine you dread will follow you into Egypt, and there you will die' " (42:9–16).

What happens next may have surprised even Jeremiah. In spite of the promises of what will be theirs if they stay where they are and let God save them, in spite of the clear delineation of the consequences of trying to save themselves, the remnant leader calls the prophet a liar! He accuses Jeremiah of collaborating with the enemy. The army officers take Jeremiah captive and lead away "all the remnant of Judah," marching off in the very direction God had told them not to go. "So they entered Egypt in disobedience to the LORD" (43:1–7).

WHAT WE KNOW SO FAR

Let's pause for a moment and review these early Bible stories about remnant people: Johanan and the disobedient remnant; Nebuchadnezzar and the defeated remnant; Hezekiah and the dismayed remnant survivors; Joseph's conniving remnant brothers; Noah and his precarious remnant family. What do these stories teach us about the remnant?

1. Biblical remnant people always are the last of an era—those who remain from a distinct period that has a particular feature or characteristic. Johanan takes to Egypt the last of the people of Judah. Nebuchadnezzar's victory announces the end of the southern kingdom. Noah is the final figure from the antediluvian world. There is a remnant at the end of every era, every period when significant change takes place. A remnant simply is a fragment of what once was, like a piece of cloth that is left over after most of the bolt has been sold.

2. Just like that remnant piece of cloth, biblical remnant people are cut from the same bolt of material as the rest of the fabric. Sometimes the original is beautiful, sturdy, and ready to be shaped. Sometimes it's unattractive and resistant. So it is with the remnant. God has only human beings to work with, and when it comes to human beings, the Bible declares that we've all sinned and fallen short of the glory of God (Romans 3:23). Even remnant people. We're all stubborn and resistant.

3. Biblical remnant people are distinguished, not by who they are or what they have accomplished, but by what God does for them and to them. God has an undying determination to take these ordinary people and give them an extraordinary mission that will help the world better understand what type of God He really is.

He's the type of God who will take an uncertain family like Noah's and make them the heirs of the righteousness that comes by faith (Hebrews 11:7).

He's a God who will take conniving brothers like Joseph's and establish them as the progenitors of *His* people, rescue them from slavery, and then picture the rescue mission like this: "I carried you on

> "They remembered that God was
>   their Rock,
>   that God Most High was
>   their Redeemer.
> But then they would flatter him with
>   their mouths,
>   lying to him with their tongues;
> their hearts were not loyal to him,
>   they were not faithful to
>   his covenant.
> Yet he was merciful;
>   he forgave their iniquities
>   and did not destroy them.
> Time after time he restrained his anger
>   and did not stir up his full wrath"
>   (Psalm 78:35–38).

eagle's wings and brought you to myself" (Exodus 19:4).

God is a poet who reminds us of His unfailing faithfulness in the face of Assyrian arrogance:

"Have you not heard?
    Long ago I ordained it.
In days of old I planned it;
    now I have brought it to pass.
      . . .
"Once more a remnant of the
    house of Judah
      will take root below and bear
      fruit above.
For out of Jerusalem will come a
    remnant,
      and out of Mount Zion a
      band of survivors.
The zeal of the LORD Almighty
    will accomplish this" (Isaiah
      37:26, 31, 32).

Notice whose zeal makes remnant people what they are.

The remnant reveals that the Lord is the type of God who will stand in front of people who are going in absolutely the wrong direction and swear to them, "I will build you up and not tear you down; I will plant you and not uproot you. . . . I am with you and will save you and deliver you" (Jeremiah 42:10, 11).

The biblical doctrine of the remnant is about the loyalty and faithfulness of God![3]

A REMNANT RETURNS FROM BABYLON

Seventy years pass after the fall of Jerusalem. The exiles in captivity in Babylon lament their lost homeland. And then a new world power takes control in the ancient Middle East.

"In the first year of Cyrus king of Persia," the king signs a proclamation permitting any Jew who chooses to do so to return to Judah and help rebuild the temple in Jerusalem (Ezra 1:1–4). The returning remnant numbers 42,360 (2:64–67). But even for that large a group, the rebuilding proves to be a difficult task, and the reconstruction project turns out to be a great disappointment. Many of the older exiles weep when they realize the obvious disparity between the new temple and the one that had stood there before (3:12).

By the time Ezra appears on the scene, the temple has been rebuilt, but already, once again, the remnant people can only be characterized by their *unfaithfulness* (9:2, 4; 10:2, 6, 10). When Ezra begins to understand the situation, he tears his clothes, pulls hair from his head and beard, and sits down "appalled" (9:3).

Now, listen carefully to the words of Ezra's prayer (9:6–15):

"O my God, I am too ashamed and disgraced to lift up my face to you, my God, because our sins are higher than our heads and our guilt has reached to the heavens. From the days of our forefathers until now, our guilt has been great. Because of our sins, we and our kings and our priests have been subjected to the sword and captivity, to pillage and humiliation at the hand of foreign kings, as it is today.

"But now, for a brief moment, the LORD our God has been gracious in leaving us a remnant and giving us a firm place in his sanctuary, and so our God gives light to our eyes and a little relief in our bondage. Though we are slaves, our God has not deserted us in our bondage. He has shown us kindness in the sight of the kings of Persia: He has granted us new life to rebuild the house of our God and repair its ruins, and he has given us a wall of protection in Judah and Jerusalem.

"But now, O our God, what can we say after this? For we have disregarded the commands you gave through your servants the prophets. . . .

"What has happened to us is a result of our evil deeds and our great guilt, and yet, our God, you have punished us less than our sins have deserved and have given us a remnant like this. Shall we again break your commands? . . . Would you not be angry enough with us to destroy us, leaving us no remnant or survivor? O LORD, God of Israel, you are righteous! We are left this day as a remnant. Here we are before you in our guilt, though because of it not one of us can stand in your presence."

Here is Ezra's description of the remnant people: "Our sins are higher than our heads." "Our guilt has reached the heavens." "We have disregarded the commands you gave through your servants the prophets." Our situation is "a result of our evil deeds and our great guilt." "Here we are before you in our guilt." "Not one of us can stand in your presence."

Doesn't sound like a very faithful and loyal group, does it?

Here, on the other hand, is Ezra's description of the God of the remnant people: "The Lord our God has been gracious in leaving us a remnant and giving us a firm place in his sanctuary." "Our God gives light to our eyes and a little relief in our bondage." "Our God has not deserted us." "He has shown us kindness." "He has granted us new life." "He has given us a wall of protection." "You have punished us less than our sins have deserved and have given us a remnant like this." "You are righteous!"

Now we're talking faithfulness and loyalty!

This remnant, this last of the era of the exiles, is a stubborn and resistant people, cut from the same fabric as those around them. Yet God remains a God of grace—Ezra says God has "punished us less than our sins have deserved." God wants these ordinary people to respond to *His kindness,* to confess their resistance to *His faithfulness,* to open their eyes to *His light,* to experience *His relief* from their bondage, to celebrate *His new life,* and to accept the extraordinary mission to tell the world that it is *His zeal* that accomplishes all this.[4]

MONUMENTS TO GOD'S MERCY

As it was in every era in which God has chosen a remnant, so it will be again in the last days of earth's history. The end-time remnant will be characterized by the same mission and message as were the remnant people in the days of Noah and Joseph, Hezekiah and Nebuchadnezzar, Jeremiah and Ezra. The end-time remnant will stand before the world as "monuments to God's mercy."[5]

"In those days, at that time,"
    declares the LORD,
"search will be made for Israel's
      guilt,
    but there will be none,
and for the sins of Judah,
    but none will be found,
    for I will forgive the remnant
      I spare" (Jeremiah 50:20).

Who is a God like you,
    who pardons sin and forgives
      the transgression
    of the remnant of his inheritance?
You do not stay angry forever
    but delight to show mercy.
You will again have compassion
      on us;
    you will tread our sins underfoot
    and hurl all our iniquities into

the depths of the sea (Micah 7:18, 19).

In that day the LORD Almighty
   will be a glorious crown,
a beautiful wreath
     for the remnant of his people
     (Isaiah 28:5).

"Who is a God like you,
   who pardons sin and forgives
     the transgression
of the remnant of his inheritance?
You do not stay angry forever
   but delight to show mercy.
You will again have compassion on us;
   you will tread our sins underfoot
   and hurl all our iniquities
     into the depths of the sea"
     (Micah 7:18, 19).

"In that day the LORD Almighty
   will be a glorious crown,
a beautiful wreath
   for the remnant of his people"
   (Isaiah 28:5).

"So too, at the present time there is a remnant chosen by grace. And if by grace, then it is no longer by works; if it were, grace would no longer be grace" (Romans 11:5, 6).

A *biblical* doctrine of the remnant must be grounded in the realities of the Bible. And when it is, the doctrine is about God, not about us. It's about God's active, zealous commitment to save us. It's about God's persistent love, His unfailing goodness, and His enduring grace. It's not about how faithful or loyal we'd like everyone to believe we are. It's not about how many commandments we keep or how many temptations we overcome. And it's certainly not about how many members our church has around the world, or how many publishing houses we maintain, or how many hospitals we own, or how many universities we operate.

The Bible's remnant doctrine helps us declare with the psalmist:

I will sing of *the LORD's great love*
   forever;
   with my mouth I will make
     your faithfulness known
     through all generations.
I will declare that *your love* stands
   firm forever,
   that you established *your*
     faithfulness in heaven itself. . . .
Righteousness and justice are the
   foundation of your throne;
   love and faithfulness go before
   you (Psalm 89:1, 2, 14).

Our part in "remnancy" is always the same: to accept God's grace. Then we declare the remnant message about the loyalty and faithfulness of our merciful God.

---

1. "We should not study the Bible for the purpose of sustaining our preconceived opinions, but with the single object of learning what God has said." Ellen G. White, *Testimonies to Ministers and Gospel Workers* (Mountain View, Calif.: Pacific Press®, 1923), 105.

2. "Of special value to God's church on earth today—the keepers of His vineyard—are the messages of counsel and admonition given through the prophets who have made plain His eternal purpose in behalf of mankind. In the teachings of the prophets, His love for the lost race, and His plan for their salvation, are clearly revealed. The story of Israel's call, of their successes and failures, of their restoration to divine favor, of their rejection of the Master of the vineyard, and of the carrying out of the plan of the ages by a goodly remnant to whom are to be fulfilled all the covenant promises,—this has been the theme of God's messengers to His church throughout the centuries that have passed. And today God's message to His church—to those who are occupying His vineyard as faithful husbandmen—is none other than that spoken through the prophet of old:

" 'Sing ye unto her,
    A vineyard of red wine.

" 'I the Lord do keep it;
    I will water it every moment:
    Lest any hurt it, I will keep it
        night and day.' Isaiah 27:2, 3.

"Let Israel hope in God. The Master of the vineyard is even now gathering from among men of all nations and peoples the precious fruits for which He has long been waiting. Soon He will come unto His own; and in that glad day, His eternal purpose for the house of Israel will finally be fulfilled. 'He shall cause them that come of Jacob to take root: Israel shall blossom and bud, and fill the face of the world with fruit.' Isa. 27:6." Ellen G. White, *Prophets and Kings* (Mountain View, Calif.: Pacific Press®, 1943), 22.

3. "The hand of the Lord is set to recover the remnant of His people, and He will accomplish the work gloriously." Ellen G. White, *Early Writings* (Washington, D.C.: Review and Herald®, 1945), 70.

4. "Jesus imparts all the powers, all the grace, all the penitence, all the inclination, all the pardon of sins, in presenting His righteousness for man to grasp by living faith—which is also the gift of God. If you would gather together everything that is good and holy and noble and lovely in man and then present the subject to the angels of God as acting a part in the salvation of the human soul or in merit, the proposition would be rejected as treason." Ellen G. White, *Faith and Works* (Nashville Tenn.: Southern Publishing Association, 1979), 24.

5. White, *Prophets and Kings*, 300.

VISION NUMBER THREE
REVELATION 14:6–12

"Then I saw another angel flying in the midst of heaven, having the everlasting gospel to preach to those who dwell on the earth—to every nation, tribe, tongue, and people—saying with a loud voice, 'Fear God and give glory to Him, for the hour of His judgment has come; and worship Him who made heaven and earth, the sea and springs of water.'

"And another angel followed, saying, 'Babylon is fallen, is fallen, that great city, because she has made all nations drink of the wine of the wrath of her fornication.'

"Then a third angel followed them, saying with a loud voice, 'If anyone worships the beast and his image, and receives his mark on his forehead or on his hand, he himself shall also drink of the wine of the wrath of God, which is poured out full strength into the cup of His indignation. He shall be tormented with fire and brimstone in the presence of the holy angels and in the presence of the Lamb. And the smoke of their torment ascends forever and ever; and they have no rest day or night, who worship the beast and his image, and whoever receives the mark of his name.'

"Here is the patience of the saints; here are those who keep the commandments of God and the faith of Jesus" (NKJV).

"Meanwhile, the saints stand passionately patient, keeping God's commands, staying faithful to Jesus" (verse 12, *The Message*).

SUDDENLY, THE PICTURE CAME ALIVE

What distinguishes the genuine from the fake? Can you tell the difference between the actual and the spurious? Between an original and a forgery?

I n the spring of 1993, Baron Frederic Rolin left his home in Brussels with a small package tucked under his arm. The baron had an appointment with Gregory Rubinstein, a specialist in the old masters of European art for the auction house Sotheby's. When the baron unwrapped the package, Rubinstein gasped.

Encased in an ornate gilded frame was a canvas just smaller than eight by ten inches in size. Rolin revealed that he had fallen in love with this little painting more than thirty years earlier when he discovered it in the studio of an art dealer in London. Rolin had come to the conclusion that none other than Johannes Vermeer, the brilliant Dutch artist who left a legacy of only thirty-five paintings, had created this small treasure around 1670.

Rubenstein admits to being "fascinated" by the superb quality of the painting, and yet to feeling somehow mysteriously disturbed by an awkwardness and a lack of subtlety in some of the shadows. "When I first saw it," he remembers, "my initial impression was one of contradictions. The composition seemed

Johannes Vermeer, *Young Woman Seated at the Virginal*
To view this painting in color, go to www.pacificpress.com/chosenbygrace.

definitively Vermeer, and there were certain passages that I simply could not imagine having been painted by anyone else. Yet Vermeer's utterly distinctive light, atmosphere, and sense of calm were somehow not entirely present."

The picture's authenticity actually had been called into question years earlier. Hidden away in the private collection of a South African–born Irish diamond magnate and then in the possession of Rolin, the painting had been unavailable for critical examination.

Following the fascinating scandal of Han van Meegeren (a Dutch art forger convicted of painting and selling seven fake Vermeers to collectors and art museums between 1937 and 1943), the leading postwar Vermeer scholars "hardly even considered the possibility that this painting might actually be genuine."

Rubinstein persuaded Baron Rolin to leave the painting with him, and for the next ten years, Rubinstein engaged in a fascinating journey of examination and discovery, "the most enthralling and engrossing research I've ever done," he assures us.

He began by taking the painting to the National Gallery in London, where it was compared with two larger Vermeer paintings. Analyzing the three paintings under a microscope, researchers compared the pigments, examined the warp and the weft of the canvas, studied the composition of the priming levels, and even investigated the hairstyle of the girl in the picture. Unfortunately, the decade of analysis, while producing intriguing suggestions about the authenticity of the painting, failed to end the debate. All the experts involved agreed that no firm or final conclusion could be reached.

Rubenstein, however, was not satisfied. In October 2002, he brought together the leading authorities in the field of art restoration to oversee a program of careful cleaning. For the next year and a half, the painstaking work took place in the Netherlands. Skilled technicians meticulously removed more than three centuries of dust and grime. With gentle puffs of air and soft cotton swabs, the workers restored the painting, millimeter by millimeter, to its original luster.

"Suddenly the picture came alive," Sotheby's curators exclaimed. "The cool, serene lighting so typical of Vermeer reappeared, and a 'new,' convincing and enchantingly characteristic work emerged. For those who saw the changes, the reemergence of this exceptional work by the most distinctive master of seventeenth-century Holland was an astonishing and moving event." The experts agreed. By late 2003, the committee's conclusion had become unanimous: the love of Baron Rolin's life was indeed an original Vermeer. It took more than a decade of dedicated work to restore "the distinctive light . . . and sense of calm." But now we are assured: this is the genuine article, as fresh and compelling as the day it came from the hand of the master artist.

In May 2004, our son Benjamin, then a graduate student in New York City, alerted us to the authentication of the Vermeer painting and to the fact that the painting would be exhibited for two weeks in Sotheby's New York. Karen and I flew east and spent several hours in Sotheby's with Ben and his wife, Jenny, viewing the painting. I'm a dedicated Vermeer fan and have as one of my life goals to see every one of what we now know to be his thirty-six paintings. I'm at twenty-six and counting! In July, this Vermeer was shipped to Sotheby's in London, where it was sold at auction to an anonymous bidder for thirty million dollars.

The buyer turned out to be Steve Wynn of Nevada, who took this Vermeer to one of his Las Vegas resort hotels. For several years it hung there, just a few hours' drive from our home in southern California. It was the only Vermeer in America west of New York City and Washington, D.C. Just recently, Wynn sold the painting again, and now it's back in New York, at the Leiden Gallery on Madison Avenue.[1]

---

1. I've garnered the details of the story of Vermeer's 1670 painting, *Young Woman Seated at the Virginal,* from Gregory Rubenstein's article "Seeing the Light," in the June/July 2004 edition of *Preview;* from Sotheby's catalog that announced the July 7, 2004, sale of the painting; from Carol Vogel's March 31, 2004, article in the *New York Times,* "A Vermeer, Once Suspect, Will Be Offered at Sotheby's"; and from the *Essential Vermeer Newsletter,* No. 15 (May 22, 2005).

CHAPTER THREE
MARKED BY GOD'S COMMANDS

Is there a distinctive light that identifies God's end-time people? If we search for the compositions of the Master Artist, can we find them? Can we know for sure?

H ere they are," John the revelator announces.

In the middle of his glorious "revelation of Jesus Christ," the prophet of Patmos points to those he is sure are authentic end-time people—"the saints." They are those who "obey God's commandments and hold to the testimony of Jesus" (Revelation 12:17; compare 14:12).

John would have argued that not everyone who merely is alive during the last days of earth's history meets the biblical qualifications for being counted as an "end-time person." From John's perspective, there are "saints" and there are "nonsaints." Obeying the commands of God and holding to the faith of Jesus are not universal attributes of people living at the end—sadly, not even among those who claim that they are obedient followers.

It's Jesus, in fact, who introduces us to a group of arrogant *religious* people who will be alive at the time of His second coming—people who boast that they have prophesied, driven out demons, and performed miracles—"many miracles"—in Christ's name. But the poignant response of Jesus is "I never knew you. Away from me you *evildoers*" (Matthew 7:21–23). Paul calls this group *blinded people* who "cannot see the light of the gospel of the glory of Christ" (2 Corinthians 4:4) and *bewitched people* who are now trying to attain their goal "by human effort" (Galatians 3:1–5). John refers to them as *led-astray people* (Revelation 12:9). Using John's unfavorable term, we'll compare the Bible's portraits of led-astray people with how it portrays end-time people.

A careful analysis of both groups—the verifiable end-time people and the arrogant led-astray people—uncovers unnerving similarities and vast differences. Both groups are the subjects of angelic proclamation. An angel says the end-time scenario is about telling the everlasting gospel to all the people of the earth, to every nation and every tribe. Another angel reports that led-astray people also have a relationship with all the nations of the world, but that the platform from which they operate is a fallen one.

Both groups worship. End-time people worship God and give Him glory. They sing praises to the One "who made the heavens, the earth, the sea and the springs of water." Led-astray people also worship. But the center of their praise turns out to be a beast, not the Creator. And the beast's future is abysmal, not eternally glorious.

Both groups are obedient. End-time people obey God's commands and teach others to do so (Matthew 28:20). Led-astray people also obey. Posturing as people of God, they perform "great signs and miracles" that are so convincing they almost deceive the saints (24:24).

THE PROMISED-LAND PRINCIPLE

Both groups also make a connection between obeying God's commands and entering the Promised Land.

End-time people obey because God

> "The LORD your God has given you the land. Go up and take possession of it" (Deuteronomy 1:21).
>
> "Go in and take possession of the land that the LORD, the God of your fathers, is giving you" (Deuteronomy 4:1).
>
> "Your guilt is taken away and your sin is atoned for. . . .
> "Here am I. Send me" (Isaiah 6:7, 8).
>
> "You did not choose me, but I chose you and appointed you to go and bear fruit" (John 15:16).

has already given the Promised Land to them. First comes God's gift, then our response. "I have given you this land. Go in and take possession of the land" (Deuteronomy 1:8). This "Promised-Land principle" is repeated over and over again in the Bible: first comes the gift, then the obedience. "I do this because of what the Lord did for me" (Exodus 13:8). "Neither do I condemn you. Go now and leave your life of sin" (John 8:11).

What's the best way to go in and possess the land that God has given us? "Keep the commands of the LORD your God" (Deuteronomy 4:2). "Be careful to do what the LORD your God has commanded you; do not turn aside to the right or to the left. Walk in all the way that the LORD your God has commanded you" (5:32, 33). "Love the LORD your God and keep his requirements, his decrees, his laws and his commands always" (11:1).

Because obedience is our response to God's gift, end-time people further understand that none of us are given the gift *because* we obey. Moses makes that clear: "It is not because of your righteousness or your integrity that you are going in to take possession of their land" (9:5). "The LORD did not set his affection on you and choose you because you were more numerous than other peoples, for you were the fewest of all peoples. But it was because the LORD loved you and kept the oath he swore to your forefathers that he brought you out with a mighty hand and redeemed you" (7:7, 8). "No one will be declared righteous in his sight by observing the law," Paul agrees (Romans 3:20). "Clearly," he continues in Galatians, "no one is justified before God by the law" (Galatians 3:11). In fact, if we *rely* on our obedience, maintaining that God will have to give us the gift because of our obedience, Paul insists that we are "under a curse" (3:10).

The people John calls led-astray also connect obedience to entering the Promised Land. But, in contradiction to the Bible's Promised-Land principle, led-astray theology elevates obedience to the role of a prior action *that elicits a response from God*! Obedience comes first, led-astray stalwarts preach, requiring—even demanding—a commensurate gift from God. If we obey, then God must reward us with the Promised Land.

Their point is unmistakable. Browse the Web sites. Read the publications. Listen to the sermons. Examine the emphases. The sound heard above all other pronouncements has to do, not with God's uncompromising grace or with His benevolent actions on our behalf, but with *our* obeying, *our* remembering, *our* keeping, *our* doing.

What is tragic about this led-astray position is that it minimizes and cheapens three foundational dynamics of salvation: the high and holy qualification for justification, the categorically disqualifying nature of sin, and the unconditional gift of God's grace.

The qualification for justification has *never* changed. The price of admission into the Promised Land, the condition of eternal life, is now just what it always has been: *Perfect* obedience to *all* God's commands. Perfect righteousness. Perfect holiness.[1] But Jesus dramatically insists that, for humans in their fallen nature, *perfect* obedience is *impossible* (Matthew 19:26;

" 'Who has ever given to God,
  that God should repay him?'
For from him and through him and
  to him are all things.
  To him be the glory forever!" (Romans
    11:35, 36).

"In him we have redemption through his blood, the forgiveness of sins, in accordance with the riches of God's grace" (Ephesians 1:7).

Mark 10:27; Luke 18:27). "All have sinned and fall short of the glory of God, and are justified freely by his grace through the redemption that came by Christ Jesus" (Romans 3:23, 24). It is *Christ's* obedience, and His obedience *alone,* that qualifies us for heaven! If salvation is any less than 100 percent free, if we can earn even a small portion of it, or merit even the slightest percentage, or contribute to any part of the Promised Land gift, then it is a cheap grace that God offers. In fact, grace is demanding, costly, and expensive—to the Giver of the gift.

No man can redeem the life of
    another
    or give to God a ransom for
      him—
  the ransom for a life is costly,
    no payment is ever enough—

that he should live on forever
  and not see decay (Psalm
    49:7–9).

Hard-working, led-astray loyalists often ask, "If our attempts to obey don't contribute to our eternal salvation, if our obedience isn't the determining condition of our justification, then why obey at all?" Another version of the question goes, "If you accept God's grace as the only ground of salvation, then why not just quit obeying altogether?" And, "If you've

"I long for your salvation, O LORD,
  and your law is my delight" (Psalm
    119:174).

"There remains, then, a Sabbath-rest for the people of God; for anyone who enters God's rest also rests from his own work, just as God did from his" (Hebrews 4:9, 10).

"Now have come the salvation and
    the power and the kingdom
    of our God,
  and the authority of his Christ.
For the accuser of our brothers,
  who accuses them before our
    God day and night,
  has been hurled down.
They overcame him
  by the blood of the Lamb" (Revelation
    12:10, 11).

really been saved already, what difference does it make if you sin?"

I've also asked these questions. I've worried that God doesn't sufficiently understand human nature. Shouldn't God motivate us by holding back just a little? What if grace ends up making us negligent on Sabbath observance, or lazy when it comes to overcoming, or gives us permission to lower our standards? Wouldn't He more effectively encourage us to progress in the spiritual life if He made things a little harder—or at least required a division of the responsibility for salvation: perhaps 75 percent on His part and 25 percent on ours?

Yet look again at those people in the Bible who acknowledge being saved by grace alone. *They don't question obedience to the commands of God!* They rejoice in the Sabbath. They experience the joy of overcoming. They know that they are justified by grace alone—and because of their changed status, they desire to respond to God's grace by obeying and overcoming and becoming more like Jesus. "They follow the Lamb wherever he goes" (Revelation 14:4).

There are two clear biblical reasons for such obedience.

OBEYING TO TESTIFY

One reason we obey is so our obedience can testify loudly and clearly about the goodness of God. Matthew says it like this: "Let your light shine before men, that they may see your good deeds and praise your Father in heaven" (Matthew 5:16). Peter says, "Live such good lives among the pagans that, though they accuse you of doing wrong, they may see your good deeds and glorify God" (1 Peter 2:12).

> "Walk in all the way that the LORD your God has commanded you, so that you may live and prosper and prolong your days in the land that you will possess" (Deuteronomy 5:33).
>
> "Observe therefore all the commands I am giving you today, so that you may have the strength to go in and take over the land that you are crossing the Jordan to possess" (Deuteronomy 11:8).

That's exactly the experience of the primitive Christian church. In Acts 2, Luke described the young followers of Jesus this way: "They devoted themselves to the apostles' teaching and to the fellowship, to the breaking of bread and to prayer. Everyone was filled with awe, and many wonders and miraculous signs were done by the apostles.

All the believers were together and had everything in common. Selling their possessions and goods, they gave to anyone as he had need" (Acts 2:42–45). Then Luke writes about their witness—about how the church's obedience to God's commands told unbelievers what was central to the church's faith. *The Message* Bible expresses it this way: "People in general liked what they saw" (2:47). Luke notes that "the Lord added to their number daily those who were being saved."

Biblical obedience has always produced this result. Abram returns from rescuing his nephew Lot, routing the combined forces of four kingdoms with just 318 men, recovering all the goods that had been stolen, and bringing back every captive who had been taken. Melchizedek, king of Salem, appraises the impossible situation, recognizes the improbable victory, and glorifies *God* for Abram's accomplishments: "Blessed be God Most High," the king exclaims, "who delivered your enemies into your hand" (Genesis 14:20).

The boy David defeats Goliath, the giant Philistine veteran of years of battle. Then he gives the credit all to God, telling the Philistines, "the whole world will know that there is a God in Israel. All those gathered here will know that it is not by sword or spear that the Lord saves; for the battle is the LORD's, and he will give all of you into our hands" (1 Samuel 17:46, 47).

Daniel lives with the remnant in Babylon and continues to uphold the values of a God-centered life. When Nebuchadnezzar is troubled by his dream of a great image, Daniel refuses to take credit for himself as a wise man. He points to the God of heaven as the One who knows the future and who reveals mysteries. After listening to the interpretation of the dream, Nebuchadnezzar responds, "Surely your God is the God of gods and the Lord of kings and a revealer of mysteries" (Daniel 2:47).

Zechariah and Elizabeth, in their old age, become the parents of the boy who will one day point to Jesus and say, "Behold the Lamb of God who takes away the sin of the world." The people in the community marvel about a God who can perform such miraculous deeds: "The neighbors were all filled with awe, and throughout the hill country of Judea people were talking about all these things. Everyone who heard this wondered about it" (Luke 1:65, 66).

Paul and Silas protect the Philippian jailer after an earthquake. The jailer responds to their kindness by asking to be baptized: "He was filled with joy because he had come to believe in God—he and his whole family" (Acts 16:22–34).

End-time obedience glorifies the Giver of the commands, not the ones doing the obeying. Whenever we turn from giving God that glory and start to think that we are loved more or have become more righteous or are closer to meriting God's gifts because we obey, we stray from the biblical position on obedience.

OBEYING FOR OUR OWN GOOD

A second reason we obey is that obeying is our way of acknowledging that God knows what He's talking about and that He asks us to do only what is best for us. "Keep his decrees and commands," Moses explains, "so that it may go well with you and your children after you and that you may live long in the land the LORD your God gives you for all time" (Deuteronomy 4:40; also see 5:29). We are convinced that our Parent God, whose children we are by His loving adoption, has our best interest in mind when He commands—so we obey!

Many have likened this dynamic to what's involved in earthly parents' restricting their children from playing in the middle of the street. When Karen's and my two oldest kids were preschool-

ers, we lived half a block from a busy intersection that was controlled by a stoplight. On the far side of the light, the traffic flowed in two lanes, while on our side of the light, those two lanes merged into one. So at the first hint of a green light, the cars on the far side roared toward our place, racing for a spot in the single lane. The furious rush and the lack of caution constituted an accident just waiting to happen. So, with the utmost love but also with the maximum insistence, Karen and I absolutely, no questions asked, restricted Erin and Matthew from wandering into the street. It's clear, isn't it, that they didn't become our children *if* they didn't play in the street? They didn't play in the street *because* they were our children.

If God says it's best for His already redeemed children to honor their parents and not kill each other (Exodus 20:12, 13), then honoring our parents and not killing each other is what we will do. If God commands His already chosen people, holy and dearly loved, to "clothe yourselves in compassion, kindness, humility, gentleness and patience" (Colossians 3:12), then, by the grace of God and the empowering of the Holy Spirit, that is exactly how we'll strive to live. If God reveals to us that He "defends the cause of the fatherless and the widow, and loves the alien, giving him food and clothing" and then instructs His children to behave like their Father (Deuteronomy 10:18, 19), then we will be careful to follow the command. "Watch yourselves closely," God tells us, "so that you do not forget the things your eyes have seen or let them slip from your heart as long as you live" (4:9). Whether it's remembering the Sabbath to keep it holy (Exodus 20:8) or not being gossipers or slanderers, arrogant or boastful (Romans 1:29, 30), we will keep God's commands. That's what end-time people do.

WHAT ARE THE COMMANDS OF GOD?

This realization of why end-time people obey God also brings into focus the breadth of their understanding of the phrase "the commands of God." For end-time people, the term is unbounded. It isn't limited to one testament or the other. It isn't restricted to one assemblage of commands while excluding others. It doesn't consist of some special something that we obey in contrast to other people who don't obey in that matter.

Without question, the phrase "the commands of God" points to the perfect law of God, the Ten Commandments—the "transcript of God's character" delivered to humans directly from the hand of God on the top of Mount Sinai (Exodus 20:2–17). "You shall have no other gods before me"; "You shall not misuse the name of the LORD your God"; "Remember the Sabbath day"—each of the commands in the Decalogue is included.

The phrase is further shaped by the commands in the book of Deuteronomy regarding how chosen people are to live: "Love the LORD your God with all your heart and with all your soul and with all your strength" (6:5). "Impress [these commands] on your children. Talk about them when you sit at home and when you walk along the road, when you lie down and when you get up" (6:7). "Do not be stiff-necked any longer" (10:16). "Do not be hardhearted or tightfisted toward your poor brother" (15:7). "Rejoice in all the good things the LORD your God has given to you" (26:11).

The phrase also encompasses the commands embedded in Jesus' sermon on the mount (Matthew 5; 6; and 7): "If someone strikes you on the right cheek, turn to him the other also" (5:39). "Love your enemies" (5:44). "Do not worry about tomorrow" (6:34). "Do not judge" (7:1), and so on. It is comprised as well by the imperatives with which Jesus concluded so many of His parables, as in Matthew 25:13, "Keep watch," and Luke 15:32, "Celebrate and be glad, because this brother of yours was dead and is alive again; he was lost and is found."

The expression "the commands of God" incorporates also the divine instructions communicated in the New Testament letters to the churches, such as Paul's "set your minds on things above, not on earthly things" (Colossians 3:2) and "in humility consider others better than yourselves" (Philippians 2:3). It includes Peter's directives to "live in harmony with one another" and to "not repay evil with evil or insult with insult" (1 Peter 3:8, 9) and the injunctions to love one another found in the epistles of John (1 John 4:7). And in Revelation, it takes in the commands in the messages to the seven churches (Revelation 2 and 3) and the implicit command to "follow the Lamb wherever he goes" (Revelation 14:4).

For end-time people, the phrase is inclusive and comprehensive. Jesus asks us to teach others "to obey *everything* I have commanded you" (Matthew 28:20). End-time people consider this "everything" to be the essential quality, the defining element in the identifying phrase "Here are those who keep the commandments of God" (Revelation 14:12, NKJV).

The full measure of the faith of end-time people is in Jesus. They know they are chosen by grace. They know that "salvation comes no other way; for no other name has been or will be given to us by which we can be saved" (Acts 4:12, *The Message*).

In grateful response, we open our lives to the guidance and the power of the Spirit, who is a gift from God (Acts 2:38; 10:45) to fill our hearts with God's love (Romans 5:5), to teach us to obey all that God commands, and to remind us of everything Jesus has revealed to us (John 14:26; cf. verse 21). The Spirit "will guide you into all truth," Jesus promises (16:13). The Spirit empowers us to be His witnesses (Acts 1:8). The Spirit gives us the gifts of ministry with which we serve others (1 Corinthians 12:4–13).

When we allow the Holy Spirit to remove the centuries of accumulated grime from our lives, when the cleansing and restoration is taking place and the original luster—"the distinctive light, the sense of calm"—is returning, people will look at us and glorify God. They'll say, "What Master Artist created such a wondrous work?"

---

1. "The condition of eternal life is now just

what it always has been,—just what it was in Paradise before the fall of our first parents,—perfect obedience to the law of God, perfect righteousness. If eternal life were granted on any condition short of this, then the happiness of the whole universe would be imperiled. The way would be open for sin, with all its train of woe and misery, to be immortalized.

"It was possible for Adam, before the fall, to form a righteous character by obedience to God's law. But he failed to do this, and because of his sin our natures are fallen, and we cannot make ourselves righteous. Since we are sinful, unholy, we cannot perfectly obey a holy law. We have no righteousness of our own with which to meet the claims of the law of God. But Christ has made a way of escape for us. He lived on earth amid trials and temptations such as we have to meet. He lived a sinless life. He died for us, and now He offers to take our sins and give us His righteousness. If you give yourself to Him, and accept Him as your Saviour, then, sinful as your life may have been, for His sake you are accounted righteous. Christ's character stands in place of your character, and you are accepted before God just as if you had not sinned." Ellen G. White, *Steps to Christ* (Mountain View, Calif.: Pacific Press®, 1943), 62.

Implications for Evangelism

Often, we've filled our evangelistic endeavors with tales of led-astray people who have attempted to change God's commands, to ignore them, or to lead others into disobeying them. What do you think would happen if instead we filled our evangelism with the stories of authentic end-time people who heroically and fruitfully are trying to obey all of God's commands?

What if, for example, instead of recounting medieval intrigues to add human works to the doctrine of salvation by grace alone, we featured testimonies of people whose lives have been changed dramatically by grace? What if rather than focusing on the claims of aged catechisms about changing the Sabbath, we focused instead on the blessings that have come our way as we have attempted to obey the Sabbath commandment?

If the biblical claim is true that people are led to glorify God when they see our obedience, our good deeds (Matthew 5:16; 1 Peter 2:12), why don't we commit to doing a better job of telling the stories of Christians who are doing good deeds: fighting AIDS in Africa, rescuing child sex-slaves in Thailand, translating the Bible into the languages of primitive tribes in South America, doing medical and dental work for refugees, and rebuilding homes for hurricane victims?

Scripture says God's kindness leads us to repentance (Romans 2:4). If that's true, might not the testimony of people who are redeemed by grace and who now are revealing the kindness of God by their obedience—might not their testimony most effectively lead people to return to their heavenly Father?

If Jesus was serious when He said, "The Son of Man must be lifted up, that everyone who believes in him may have eternal life" (John 3:14, 15), wouldn't lifting up Jesus always be a better evangelistic strategy than attempting to put down or discredit religious organizations other than our own? Isn't the good news that we are commissioned to tell to "all nations" (Matthew 28:19) really about "the Lamb that was slain from the creation of the world" (Revelation 13:8) and not about the beast that at the end of time is thrown into the lake of fire?

Vision Number Four
Ephesians 2:1–9

"As for you, you were dead in your transgressions and sins, in which you used to live when you followed the ways of this world and of the ruler of the kingdom of the air, the spirit who is now at work in those who are disobedient. All of us also lived among them at one time, gratifying the cravings of our sinful nature and following its desires and thoughts. Like the rest, we were by nature objects of wrath.

"But because of his great love for us, God, who is rich in mercy, made us alive with Christ even when we were dead in transgressions—it is by grace you have been saved. And God raised us up with Christ and seated us with him in the heavenly realms in Christ Jesus, in order that in the coming ages he might show the incomparable riches of his grace, expressed in his kindness to us in Christ Jesus.

"For it is by grace you have been saved, through faith—and this not from yourselves, it is the gift of God."

HE MOVED INTO THE NEIGHBORHOOD

How do most people picture Jesus? Is He merely a quotable revolutionary who lived two thousand years ago? Is He primarily a figment of prophetic vision? Or does He belong to us as well as to the people of Bible times? Is Jesus alive and well in our day?

Few people who lived during the Middle Ages managed to visit biblical sites in the Holy Land. Among medieval Europeans, even had they wanted to visit Bible sites, pilgrimages were just not practical. That was doubly true for the citizens of the great, populous civilizations of India and China and the more geographically bound nations in South America and Africa.

What's more, there were, obviously, no touristy Web sites on which to glimpse photographs of the foreign landscapes. There were no published drawings by someone who had been there. There were no organized tours on which you could fly to Cairo, explore the sites there, and then find your way north by train or air-conditioned bus to Amman and Jerusalem, enjoying the scenery along the way. With the tragic exceptions of the dismal twelfth- and thirteenth-century crusades against Muslims, infidels, and dissident Christians (that cost the lives of hundreds of thousands and perhaps even millions of people), travel to the Holy Land was simply out of the question.

So how did medieval European artists perceive the Egypt of Moses and the pharaohs? What did they imagine that it looked like? How about King David's capital city of Jerusalem? Or Mount Carmel? Or the little town of Bethlehem? Or the Sea of Galilee? Not even the most highly respected painters on the continent had the faintest idea.

What's more, the people who financed medieval art really didn't care. The wealthy patrons who kept artists employed wanted to see their own portraits in the paintings. They wanted certain colors to predominate. (Decorating decisions, no doubt.) They often stated their preferences for how the frame was to be made. They specified how much they were willing to pay and when they wanted the artwork delivered. But as far as the landscape, there seldom were any stipulations.

Consequently, artists didn't spend a lot of time painting landscapes. A distant vague shape sufficed for a hillside or a mountain. Squiggly blue lines were good enough for the waves on the seashore. Indistinct contours were adequate for trees, although no one would have been able to guess what type of fruit would fall from the branches. And if the painting was supposed to depict a *sacred* scene, a Bible story, what better way to express the holiness of the setting, they thought, than to cover the background with gold paint. Without any other distinguishable characteristic, the gold color would certainly convey a sense of holiness, wouldn't it? Why do anything more precise?

It is exactly that common imprecision that makes Konrad Witz's mid-fifteenth-century landscape so remarkable. In 1444, when the people of Geneva witnessed the unveiling of Witz's painting *The Miraculous Draft of Fishes,* they gasped. No one had ever seen anything like it before.

The artist had painted the scene of the risen Savior revealing Himself to seven of His disciples one morning by the Sea of Galilee (John 21:1–14). Remember that the disciples had spent the night laboring at their old occupation of fishing, but to no avail—the catch was meager and disappointing. Jesus quietly fixed breakfast for His friends, then called to them from the shore and told them to throw their net on the other side of the boat. When the disciples, who had not yet realized that it was Jesus, followed His advice, "they were unable to haul the net in because of the large number of fish" (John 21:6).

Witz captures the moment in the story when John, suddenly recognizes Jesus and shouts to the others, "It's the Lord!" and all the fishing abruptly comes to a standstill.

Konrad Witz, *The Miraculous Draft of Fishes*
To view this painting in color, go to www.pacificpress.com/chosenbygrace.

Peter stops in the middle of tugging on the net, tilts his head upward to get a better view, and looks across the lake into the eyes of Jesus.

Witz captures the very next moment too—picturing Peter a second time in the painting. In this portrayal of the disciple, he's jumped into the water and is swimming as fast as he can straight to his Friend and Master. It is clear from the look on his face, however, that while he's eager to greet Jesus, he's also recalling that just a few days ago he denied even knowing Him. How will Jesus react this morning?

A regal Jesus stands on the Galilee shore with His arms folded. He is covered with a luxuriant, flowing red robe. His head is encircled with a striking, ornate nimbus, surely one of the most creative haloes in the history of biblical art.

But it's not the inventive halo, nor the predicament of Peter, nor the dazzling red robe that made the viewers gasp. What made them catch their breath was the *background* of the painting. For the first time in Western art, someone had painted a *recognizable* landscape. And, most astonishing, it isn't Palestine's little Sea of Galilee that Witz painted. It's Lake Geneva in Switzerland. Witz has placed Jesus in a local setting!

With awe, the people of Geneva gazed at their well-known locale. There, on the right side of the painting, were the structures that actually were right over there. There was that unmistakable little white tower on the far side of the lake. There was the shallow fence that channeled the fish in toward the shore. And way in the background, that's Mont Blanc. And over there, the Salève.[1]

Witz's radical innovation was stunning, and its spiritual message is unmistakable. The Bible story is more than just history—it's pertinent, meaningful, and applicable to us in our place and in our time. The miracle of the fishes, like all the other surprising wonders of God, can happen here and now. Jesus is not just a pleasing narrative from an ancient Testament. He's not just an apocalyptic vision of a one-of-these-days Commander riding a white horse at the front of the armies of heaven. He's nearby, contemporary, and accessible!

What do you think would happen if we always pictured Jesus in our local settings? "The Word became flesh and blood / and moved into the neighborhood," *The Message* Bible interprets John 1:14. What if we always showed the Son of God in our neighborhoods, at work in our part of the world, conversing with and ministering to people just like you and me, addressing the same issues that challenge us today?

A few years ago a series of drawings appeared in *Insight* magazine showing Jesus in present-day circumstances—reading a newspaper, watching a couple of teenage boys paint the side of a house, picking up a puppy that had been hit by a car. One reader of the magazine, outraged at the modern depiction of Christ, wrote an angry letter to the editor saying, "How dare you picture Jesus in a contemporary setting?"

Shouldn't the question be, "How dare we not?"

---

1. For this story, see Florian Heine, *The First Time: Innovations in Art* (Munich, Germany: Bucher, 2007), 66–69.

CHAPTER FOUR
MADE ALIVE IN CHRIST

How central is Jesus in the lives of end-time people? What purpose is served at the close of earth's history by the story of what Jesus has done in the lives of the redeemed? How bothered do you think our enemy might be by our testimony that we have been saved by grace?

John identifies authentic end-time people as those who obey the commands of God and hold to the testimony of Jesus (Revelation 12:17; 14:12; 19:10). We've taken a close look at what it means to obey everything God commands. Now, let's explore what the Bible has to say about "the testimony of Jesus."

The Scriptures speak strongly about the importance of truthful testimony. Proverbs 12:17 contrasts having an "honest testimony" with giving "a false witness," an act strictly forbidden in the Ten Commandments (Exodus 20:16), right up there with not stealing and not murdering, not coveting and not breaking the Sabbath. Luke tells us that the apostles spoke only of what they knew to be true when they "continued to testify to the resurrection of the Lord Jesus" (Acts 4:33). In the words of Jesus Himself: "I tell you the truth, we speak of what we know, and we testify to what we have seen" (John 3:11). Whatever Revelation is describing about end-time people, whatever it is that end-time people are supposed to testify about Jesus, it must be truthful.

In giving this testimony about Jesus, it isn't enough to tell someone else's truth—to say only what my mother believed, for example, or what the church taught me, or what a college religion teacher said. That's false testimony because it isn't *my* testimony. All these things inform my testimony and are part of my journey, but what I say must be about my own experience with Jesus, not about anyone else's—about what I know and what I have seen (John 1:32).

Are you a joyful follower of Jesus? Then testify about your joy. Has your experience with

Jesus been distant? It's perfectly OK to say so. Have you struggled with the theology of a divine/human Savior? Some of the greatest minds in religious history have grappled with the issue—it's good to wrestle with God. Was there a time when you finally began to grasp how important this Jesus is to your life? Are you growing in grace? That's what questioning people need to hear. Millions have told their story truthfully and in doing so have testified about Jesus.

John the Baptist testified about Jesus. He announced that Jesus was the Light of the world, shining in darkness (John 1:4–8). The Samaritan woman testified about Jesus. She convinced her village that Jesus was worth listening to, and soon they believed "that this man really is the Savior of the world" (John 4:42). John the disciple testified about Jesus. "We have seen and testify," he tells us, "that the Father has sent his Son to be the Savior of the world" (1 John 4:14). Paul testified about Jesus. In fact, Paul defined his entire ministry as testifying. "I consider my life worth nothing to me," he says honestly, "if only I may finish the race and complete the task the Lord Jesus has given me—the task of testifying to the gospel of God's grace" (Acts 20:24).

Testifying about Jesus. The Light of the world. The Savior of the world. The

One who forgives. Testifying "to the gospel of God's grace." According to Jesus, that's the testimony that will precede the end times: "This gospel of the kingdom will be preached in the whole world as a testimony to all nations, and then the end will come" (Matthew 24:14).

But if you need something even bigger, even more convincing, listen to who else gives this testimony. "God's testimony is greater," John insists, "because it is the testimony of God, which he has given about his Son. Anyone who believes in the Son of God has this testimony in his heart. Anyone who does not believe God has made him out to be a liar, because he has not believed the testimony God has given about his Son" (1 John 5:9, 10).

And what exactly is God's testimony? John answers precisely. "This is the testi-

"I do not set aside the grace of God, for if righteousness could be gained through the law, Christ died for nothing!" (Galatians 2:21).

"God has given us eternal life, and this life is in his Son" (1 John 5:11).

"Because of his great love for us, God, who is rich in mercy, made us alive with Christ even when we were dead in transgressions—it is by grace you have been saved" (Ephesians 2:4, 5).

mony: God has given us eternal life, and this life is in his Son. He who has the Son has life; he who does not have the Son of God does not have life" (5:11, 12).

This full-throated New Testament testimony of Jesus finds its sure counterpart in Old Testament symbolism. Moses called the two tablets of stone on which the finger of God had inscribed the Ten Commandments "the tablets of the Testimony" (Exodus 31:18). Moses placed those tablets in "the tabernacle of the Testimony" (38:21), in the Most Holy Place, in "the ark of the Testimony" (40:5). When God communicated directly with the people, they heard His voice speaking to them "from between the two cherubim above the atonement cover on the ark of the Testimony" (Numbers 7:89).

The commandments. The tabernacle. The ark. And above the cover of the ark, the mercy seat. Now notice this commentary on the symbolism: "The law of God, enshrined within the ark, was the great rule of righteousness and judgment. That law pronounced death upon the transgressor; but above the law was the mercy-seat, upon which the presence of God was revealed, and from which, by virtue of the atonement, pardon was granted to the repentant sinner. Thus in the work of Christ for our redemption, symbolized by the

sanctuary service, 'mercy and truth are met together; righteousness and peace have kissed each other' (Psalm 85:10)."[1]

> "Paul, a servant of Christ Jesus, called to be an apostle and set apart for the gospel of God—the gospel he promised beforehand through his prophets in the Holy Scriptures" (Romans 1:1–3).
>
> "I stand here and testify," Paul says to King Agrippa, but "I am saying nothing beyond what the prophets and Moses said would happen" (Acts 26:22).
>
> "A righteousness from God, apart from law, has been made known, to which the Law and the Prophets testify. This righteousness from God comes through faith in Jesus Christ to all who believe. There is no difference, for all have sinned and fall short of the glory of God, and are justified freely by his grace through the redemption that came by Christ Jesus" (Romans 3:21–24).

THE TESTIMONY OF JESUS

To hold to the testimony of Jesus means that we "fix our eyes on Jesus, the author and perfecter of our faith" (Hebrews 12:2), that we fully "put our faith in Christ Jesus" (Galatians 2:16), and that we place our confidence in Christ's atonement and accept God's pardon.

To hold to the testimony of Jesus means that we approach the Bible looking for and expecting to find a Christ-filled story and a Christ-centered theology. The Scriptures "are able to make you wise for salvation through faith in Christ Jesus" (2 Timothy 3:15). The "Scriptures . . . testify about me," Jesus told the Pharisees (John 5:39).

To hold to the testimony of Jesus means to "be found *in him,* not having a righteousness of my own that comes from the law, but that which is through faith in Christ— the righteousness that comes from God and is by faith" (Philippians 3:9). It means once and for all to stop our futile attempts to add our own work to the finished work of Christ. It means to bow before the throne of grace so that "grace might reign through righteousness to bring eternal life through Jesus Christ our Lord" (Romans 5:21). To hold to the testimony of Jesus means to accept God's gift of salvation. It means to rejoice that God has called us to be "a remnant chosen by grace" (Romans 11:5).

To hold to the testimony of Jesus means that we establish Jesus as the living center of all we believe, all we do, all we are. "We preach Christ crucified," Paul declares (1 Corinthians 1:23). It means that we resolve to know nothing apart from this fundamental truth (2:2). It means that we find in Jesus "the great truth around which all other truths cluster,"[2] that we present Jesus in the Creation, Jesus in the Sabbath, Jesus in the sanctuary service, Jesus in salvation, Jesus in the end times, Jesus in the remnant, Jesus in the Second Coming—that we know every truth from Genesis to Revelation "as it is in Jesus."[3]

The hymn writer captured it well:

My faith has found a resting
   place,
not in a man-made creed;
I trust the ever-living One
that He for me will plead.

I need no other evidence;
I need no other plea;
It is enough that Jesus died
and rose again for me.[4]

THE SPIRIT OF PROPHECY

The author of Revelation further maintains that holding to the testimony of Jesus is the essential quality, the venerable attribute of all the prophets throughout the ages of history, all those who have been "carried along by the Holy Spirit" (2 Peter 1:19–21). Proclaiming the everlasting gospel of God's grace (Revelation 14:6), telling the story of Jesus, the Savior of the world, John says, is "the spirit of prophecy" (19:10). To testify about Jesus is the essence of all prophetic utterance.[5]

Peter explains, "All the prophets testify about him that everyone who believes in him receives forgiveness of sins through his name" (Acts 10:43). "Concerning this salvation," Peter repeats later, "the prophets, who spoke of the grace that was to come to you, searched intently and with the greatest care" (1 Peter 1:10).

All the prophets whose lips have been touched by a cleansing coal from the heavenly altar glorify the great and Holy God who reveals "deep and hidden things" (Daniel 2:22). But there is a larger purpose for this revealing of mysteries. Far beyond just exalting the God who "knows what lies in darkness" (2:22), prophecy builds our trust in our heavenly Parent, in order that when He says to us, "your guilt is taken away and your sin atoned for" (Isaiah 6:1–7), we will believe in His sure word. God exercises His *revealing* power in order to establish our confidence in His *saving* power. Nothing else the prophet says is more important than this. Nothing less will measure up to the exalted standard: "The testimony of Jesus is the spirit of prophecy."

In the end times as well as in the former times, God pours out His Spirit on His servants, the prophets. "Your sons and

"Let heaven and earth praise him, / the seas and all that move in them" (Psalm 69:34).

"Blessed is he whose help is the
  God of Jacob,
    whose hope is in the Lord his God,
the Maker of heaven and earth,
    the sea, and everything in them—
    the Lord, who remains faithful
      forever" (Psalm 146:5, 6).

"He who builds his lofty palace in
  the heavens
    and sets its foundation on the earth,
who calls for the waters of the sea
    and pours them out over the face
      of the land—
    the Lord is his name" (Amos 9:6).

daughters will prophesy," the prophet Joel tells us. Are those end-time prophecies just to "show wonders in the heavens and on the earth," just to reveal what will happen in the last days? No! The prophets tell us these things so that "everyone who calls / on the name of the Lord will be saved" (Joel 2:28–32). "Now to him who is able to establish you by my gospel and the proclamation of Jesus Christ, according to the revelation of the mystery hidden for long ages past, but now revealed and made known through the prophetic writings by the command of the eternal God, *so that all nations might believe and obey him*—to the only wise God be glory forever through Jesus Christ! Amen" (Romans 16:25–27).

BABYLON IS FALLEN

On the remote island of Patmos, John is wondering about the end times, about "what must soon take place" as amplified by "the revelation of Jesus Christ" (Revelation 1:1). His thoughts swirl around the Lamb standing on Mount Zion. He hears the new songs that only the redeemed can sing (14:1–4). He sees three angels soaring through the heavens and listens as they tell the everlasting gospel, warn about God's wrath, and announce the judgment hour (14:6–12). The first of the three angels exhorts us to worship the Creator. The second angel declares, "Babylon the Great is fallen." The third angel describes the end of those who worship "the beast." The tabernacle of the Testimony is opened in heaven (15:5). Plagues descend to earth (15:6–16:21). Demons scatter across the globe (16:13, 14). Kings gather in Armageddon (16:16). A voice from heaven cries out, "It is done!" Thunder and lightning punctuate the drama. The most powerful earthquake in history rattles the planet's foundations (16:18). The islands "flee away" and the mountains disappear (16:20).

Suddenly, John's end-time visions are interrupted. An angel appears and "in the Spirit" carries him into a desert (17:1–3). John sees a woman sitting on a scarlet beast. The angel tells John that the woman's name is "BABYLON THE GREAT, THE MOTHER OF PROSTITUTES AND OF THE ABOMINATIONS OF THE EARTH." (17:3–6).

"She has become a home for
     demons
and a haunt for every evil spirit. . . .
. . . All the nations have drunk
     the maddening wine of her
     adulteries."

And she is fallen (18:1–3). Another angel cries out, "Come out of her, my people, / so that you will not share in her sins" (18:4). Babylon responds. "I sit as a queen," she boasts in the face of the angel's words. "I am not a widow / and I will never mourn" (18:7). "Woe, O great city, / O Babylon," the people in the vision remark. "In one hour your doom has come. . . . In one hour such great wealth has been brought to ruin" (18:10, 17).

John knows this name *Babylon*. The second angel already has announced that Babylon "is fallen." And John has come across these words before in his study of the Scriptures. But something is different now. "Babylon is fallen. . . ." "Every evil spirit . . ." "All the nations . . ." "All who have been killed on the earth . . ." (18:24). The heavens shout an authoritative declaration. The voices of the earth respond. The sea echoes the judgment.

This is not about Nimrod's city, John realizes; not about that mighty warrior who founded Babylon shortly after the Flood (Genesis 10:8–12). This is not about Nebuchadnezzar's kingdom, or the neo-Babylonian army that broke down the walls of Jerusalem, destroyed Solomon's temple, and put an end to the kingdom of Judah (2 Kings 25). This is not about that riverbank where the remnant from Judah hung their harps on the willow branches and sat down and wept (Psalm 137:1–4). The city of Babylon and the nation of Babylon and the power of Babylon all had fallen centuries earlier, long before John, before Rome, before Greece, before Persia. This is larger than all that. This is universal: the heavens, the earth, the sea, and everything in them.

These are words that God has used to remind us of the territory over which He is sovereign: "In six days the LORD made the heavens and the earth, the sea, and all that is in them" (Exodus 20:11).

Here's how angels talk about the rightful object of our worship: "Worship him who made the heavens, the earth, the sea and the springs of water" (Revelation 14:7). Here's how they speak of the events that involve the entire planet: "Then the angel I had seen standing on the sea and on the land raised his right hand to heaven. And he swore by him who lives for ever and ever, who created the heavens and all that is in them, the earth and all that is in it, and the sea and all that is in it, and said, 'There will be no more delay!' " (10:5, 6).

This is the way giants of the Old Testament refer to the God of all things: "Let the heavens rejoice, let the earth be glad; / let the sea resound, and all that is in it" (Psalm 96:11). "You alone are the LORD. You made the heavens, even the highest heavens, and all their starry host, the earth and all that is on it, the seas and all that is in them" (Nehemiah 9:6).

These are words appropriated from Isaiah: a man arrives in a chariot shouting, "Babylon has fallen, has fallen! / All the images of its gods lie shattered on the ground!" (Isaiah 21:9). Babylon said to herself,

" 'I will never be a widow
　　or suffer the loss of children.'
Both of these will overtake you
　　in a moment,"

the prophet promises, " 'on a single day' " (47:8, 9).

These are phrases taken from Jeremiah's visions: Babylon

"made the whole earth drunk.
The nations drank her wine;
    therefore they have now gone
    mad.
Babylon will suddenly fall and be
    broken" (Jeremiah 51:7, 8).

"Come out of her my people!
    Run for your lives!" (51:45).

"Then heaven and earth and all
    that is in them
    will shout for joy over Baby-
    lon,
for out of the north
    destroyers will attack her"
    (51:48).

"The slain in all the earth
have fallen because of Baby-
    lon" (51:49).

There's promise here as well as warning. Babylon is also the place where God's oppressed and plundered people from every nation on earth realize that they are "the apple of his eye," where He intervenes, where the Incarnation takes place in our neighborhoods, where Christ leads His people to their escape (Zechariah 2:7–9). Babylon is where "the Lord will redeem you / out of the hand of your enemies" (Micah 4:10).

This Babylon is larger than history. Its nomenclature is cosmic. It is ubiquitous—everywhere present in time and place; it infuses "the whole earth." It's pervasive and all-encompassing, involving "all the nations." It's about heaven, earth, and sea, and everything that is in them. Whatever else Babylon means to us, whatever other applications we give to the name, we must recognize as basic that here, in the revelation given to John, Babylon is the epicenter of all evil, the dominating, pivotal core in the war against the testimony of Jesus. If holding to the testimony of Jesus means clinging to God's gift of eternal life in His Son (1 John 5:11, 12), then Babylon represents all the hostilities, all the combat, all the antagonism, all the subterfuge of the devil marshaled against the gospel of grace.

WAR AGAINST THE TESTIMONY OF JESUS

Make no mistake about it—holding to the testimony of Jesus is a serious, dangerous position to take in the great controversy. We've been warned: "The thought that the righteousness of Christ is imputed to us, not because of any merit on our part, but as a free gift from God, is a precious thought. The enemy of God and [humankind] is not willing that this truth should be clearly presented; for he knows that if the people receive it fully, his power will be broken."[6]

Frantic at the thought of losing his power, the enemy musters the full array of his arsenal against the testimony of Jesus. From the earliest times, the dragon has waged "war" against "those who obey God's commandments and hold to the testimony of Jesus" (Revelation 12:17). John looks closely. Babylon is drunk. The angel explains: she's been drinking "the blood of those who bore testimony to Jesus" (17:6).

John is astonished. He considers his imprisonment on Patmos to be a high calling, a providence that has placed him in a position to write "what is now and what will take place later" (Revelation 1:19). But he also knows that his exile is a direct result "of the word of God and the testimony of Jesus" (1:9). Here on Patmos, John is a "companion in the suffering" of the saints.

The writer of Hebrews recalls that suffering. He looks back on the fury of flames and the edge of the sword, imprisonment, destitution, persecution, and mistreatment. He remembers God's people wandering in deserts and mountains and living in caves and holes in the ground (Hebrews 11:34–38). Paul looks this "trouble" in the eye, expands the word to include hardship, famine, nakedness, danger, and sword, and then confidently proclaims that "neither death nor life, neither angels nor demons, neither the present nor the future, nor any powers, neither height nor depth, nor anything else in all creation, will be able to separate us from the love of God that is in Christ Jesus our Lord" (Romans 8:35–39).

In answering the disciples' questions about the last days, Jesus warns about "false Christs" (Matthew 24:24). "Many will come in my name," He predicts, "claiming, 'I am the Christ' " (24:5). *Christ* is a title that designates the One anointed to be the Redeemer, the Savior of the world, the One to whom God directs our attention as the Messiah who will "bring all things in heaven and on earth together under one head, even Christ" (Ephesians 1:10). Jesus alerts us to our need to be on guard against Babylon, against the weaponry of our enemy that includes all the people, theories, doctrines, practices, and systems that divert our eyes from Him who *alone* is the source of our salvation (Psalm

62:1, 2). He cautions us that any time we add our works, our merits, or our faith to what He *alone* has accomplished to save us, we are buying into a "false christ," a false redeemer. We are accepting the rule of Babylon.

If we allow our eyes to stray from Jesus, what happens to our testimony? If our trust is not fully in the saving power of Jesus, then our focus, our faith, shifts to Babylon. When we set aside the grace of Christ, we transfer our citizenship to Babylon. Whenever we suggest that what we do or do not do, what we believe or reject, makes any contribution at all to our salvation, we stand on the platform of Babylon. We chisel away at the perfect testimony of God's love. We diminish what Jesus has done for us. We raise our own cross on Mount Calvary.

Knowing that our self-exaltation fades in the presence of the Savior, the prophets amplify their praise.

> Surely God is my salvation;
> I will trust and not be afraid.
> The LORD, the LORD, is my
> strength and my song;
> he has become my salvation
> (Isaiah 12:2).

My soul finds rest in God alone;

> my salvation comes from
> him.
> He alone is my rock and my salvation;
> he is my fortress, I will never be
> shaken (Psalm 62:1, 2).

Babylon is fallen.

Those who hold to the testimony of Jesus cannot be shaken.

---

1. Ellen G. White, *Patriarchs and Prophets* (Mountain View, Calif.: Pacific Press®, 1958), 349.

2. Ellen G. White, *Gospel Workers* (Washington, D.C.: Review and Herald,® 1948), 315.

3. Ibid., 120; cf. 156ff.

4. Lidle H. Edmunds, *My Faith Has Found a Resting Place,* around 1891.

5. See the addendum that follows this chapter.

6. White, *Gospel Workers,* 161.

It is fair for believers today to apply the Christological standard to each of the Bible prophets: Does Miriam the prophetess (Exodus 15:20) testify about Jesus? Does Samuel the prophet (1 Samuel 3:20) testify about Jesus? How about Nathan the prophet (2 Samuel 7:2), and Deborah the prophetess (Judges 4:4), and Isaiah (Isaiah 37:2), and Habakkuk (Habakkuk 1:1), and Philip's daughters (Acts 21:9), and John (Revelation 1:3)? Do they all "testify about him that everyone who believes in him receives forgiveness of sins through his name" (Acts 10:43)?

Seventh-day Adventists also apply this standard to Ellen White. She says, "Of all confessing Christians, Seventh-day Adventists should be foremost in uplifting Christ before the world" (*Gospel Workers,* 156).

"Let the science of salvation be the burden of every sermon, the theme of every song. Let it be poured forth in every supplication. Bring nothing into your preaching to supplement Christ, the wisdom and power of God. Hold forth the word of life, presenting Jesus as the hope of the penitent and the stronghold of every believer. Reveal the way of peace to the troubled and the despondent, and show forth the grace and completeness of the Saviour" (Ibid., 160).

"I present before you the great, grand monument of mercy and regeneration, salvation and redemption—the Son of God uplifted on the cross. This is to be the foundation of every discourse given by our ministers" (Ibid., 315).

"Christ and His righteousness—let this be our platform, the very life of our faith" (*Review and Herald,* August 31, 1905).

Early in her ministry, as Ellen White considered the lack of a focus on Christ that was the reality of "many who profess the name of Christ and claim to be looking for His speedy coming," she wrote: "Oh, what love, what wondrous love, hath the Son of God for us poor sinners! Should we be stupid and careless while everything is being done for our salvation that can be done? All heaven is interested for us. We should be alive and awake to honor, glorify, and adore the high and lofty One. Our hearts should flow out in love and gratitude to Him who has been so full of love and compassion to us. With our lives we should honor Him, and with pure and holy conversation show that we are born from above, that this world is not our home, but that we are pilgrims and strangers here, traveling to a better country" (*Early Writings,* 113).

"Many had lost sight of Jesus. They needed to have their eyes directed to His divine person, His merits, and His changeless love for the human family. All power is given into His hands, that He may dispense rich gifts unto [all], imparting the priceless gift of His own righteousness to the helpless human agent. This is the message that God commanded to be given to the world. It is the third angel's message, which is to be proclaimed with a loud voice, and attended with the outpouring of His Spirit in a large measure. . . . For years the church has been looking to [humans], and expecting much from [them], but not looking to Jesus, in whom our hopes of eternal life are centered. Therefore God gave to His servants a testimony that presented the truth as it is in Jesus, which is the third angel's message, in clear, distinct lines" (*Testimonies to Ministers,* 91–93).

VISION NUMBER FIVE
JOEL 2:1, 2, 11–13, 21–23, 28–32

"Blow the trumpet in Zion;
    sound the alarm on my holy hill.
Let all who live in the land tremble,
    for the day of the LORD is coming.
It is close at hand—
    a day of darkness and gloom,
    a day of clouds and blackness.
Like dawn spreading across the mountains
    a large and mighty army comes,
such as never was of old
    nor ever will be in ages to come. . . .
"The LORD thunders
    at the head of his army;
his forces are beyond number,
    and mighty are those who obey his command.
The day of the LORD is great;
    it is dreadful.
    Who can endure it?
" 'Even now,' declares the LORD,
    'return to me with all your heart,
    with fasting and weeping and mourning.'
Rend your heart
    and not your garments.

Return to the LORD your God,

> for he is gracious and compassionate,

slow to anger and abounding in love,

> and he relents from sending calamity. . . .

> "Be not afraid, O land;

> be glad and rejoice.

Surely the LORD has done great things.

> Be not afraid, O wild animals,

> for the open pastures are becoming green.

The trees are bearing their fruit;

> the fig tree and the vine yield their riches.

Be glad, O people of Zion,

> rejoice in the LORD your God,

for he has given you

> the autumn rains in righteousness.

He sends you abundant showers,

> both autumn and spring rains, as before. . . .

" 'And afterward,

> I will pour out my Spirit on all people.

Your sons and daughters will prophesy,

> your old men will dream dreams,

> your young men will see visions.

Even on my servants, both men and women,

> I will pour out my Spirit in those days.

I will show wonders in the heavens

> and on the earth,

> blood and fire and billows of smoke.

The sun will be turned to darkness

> and the moon to blood

> before the coming of the great and dreadful day of the LORD.

And everyone who calls

> on the name of the LORD will be saved.' "

THE OBJECT OF GOD'S UNCONDITIONAL ACCEPTANCE

How deep is the tragedy caused by the horrors of planet Earth's times of trouble? What is the source of our inhumane treatment of other human beings? How does God bridge the gulf that separates His stumbling creatures from His infinite love?

At four-thirty in the afternoon of Monday, April 26, 1937, German air force planes began bombing the small city of Guernica in the Basque region of northern Spain. Guernica was a stronghold of opposition forces during the Spanish Civil War (1936–1939). In the three-hour attack, three-quarters of the city's buildings were completely destroyed. Countless residents were injured, and perhaps as many as sixteen hundred were killed in the bombing or gunned down as they fled, according to initial reports.

To the supporters of those who had been attacked, the destruction of the town and its citizens took on larger-than-life significance. Guernica became the archsymbol of Fascist barbarity. By the first of May, newspapers around the world were carrying reports of the massacre accompanied by grim black-and-white photographs of the attack and the subsequent

Pablo Picasso, *Guernica*
To view this painting in color, go to www.pacificpress.com/chosenbygrace.

burning of the city. In Paris, a million protesters gathered in the streets, shouting their outrage and venting their anger.

Before the bombing, the Spanish government had invited Pablo Picasso to represent Spain in the 1937 World's Fair to be held in Paris by creating a painting that would be exhibited in the Spanish Pavilion. Picasso attended the Paris protests and then rushed back to his studio and began painting. For one full month, from May 1 to June 4, 1937, the passionate painter worked feverishly to complete the assignment.

Picasso chose to produce a monumental mural measuring a massive twelve feet high and thirty feet long. He called the painting—done in stark and dramatic shades of black and white—*Guernica*. Today, the painting resides permanently in the Queen Sofia Art Center and National Museum in Madrid.

Even at first glance, the painting is a powerful meditation on suffering and death, violence and brutality. In his distinctive, disjointed style, Picasso created images that are coarse, agonizingly broken, almost difficult to observe. You want to just walk away and find something more pleasant to view—a whimsical little piece by Joan Miró perhaps, or even a surreal distraction by Salvador Dali. But *Guernica* reaches out and grabs you and demands that you stand still and look and try to grasp the monstrous struggle and the fierce emotion.

Nothing about the painting identifies the conflict in Spain. There are no bombs or airplanes. No soldiers. The only weapon is a broken sword clenched in the grasp of a fallen man whose eyes look out unblinking from his round, hairless head, no longer seeing or recognizing anything. Men and women run in panic, with powerful legs propelling them away from the horror. One figure screams at the dark sky above him, attempting to grab the enemy and hurl them to the ground.

At the left-hand edge of *Guernica* is a woman clutching a child who has been killed in the bombing. The woman's head is thrust backward, her mouth is open in a lament of grief, and her eyes stare into the sky, from where the explosive weapons of death descended. One cannot help but feel with her the fierce rage and intense torment of losing her child in such a senseless act of extreme violence.

Guernica's power grows. The longer you stand in front of it and the more you concentrate on the bleak images, the more you feel the cry of indignation and horror. One observer says the painting has become an antiwar symbol—"a perpetual reminder of the tragedies of war." Others call it "an apocalyptic vision that serves as a banner of freedom and democracy," "the century's most unsettling indictment of war," and "the most powerful invective against violence in modern art." The painting is the subject of more books than any other piece of modern art and is often called "the most important work of art of the twentieth century."

At the Spanish Pavilion in Paris, the painting was exhibited along with photographs of soldiers fighting in the Spanish Civil War. Next to the photos were these words: "We are fighting for the essential unity of Spain. We are fighting for the integrity of Spanish soil. We are fighting for the independence of our country and for the right of the Spanish people to determine their own destiny."

During the Second World War, Picasso was living in Nazi-controlled Paris. From time to time, members of the Gestapo would visit his apartment and harass him for his art. On one occasion, the story is told, a Nazi officer saw a photo of *Guernica* and, with great disdain, asked Picasso, "Did you do that?"

"No," Picasso replied coldly, "you did."[1]

The human tragedy experienced in times of trouble is almost too horrible to speak of. How do we comprehend the depths of grief that a loving mother experiences at the loss of *one* child? How can we express the physical and mental anguish endured by *one* individual who has been beaten, tortured, or wounded in battle? And what does that level of barbaric behavior do to those who inflict the wounds, engage in the torture, or cause the death? Remove the by-now-familiar, desensitizing statistics that inure us to the suffering and anguish (thousands killed in wars and insurrections, hundreds gunned down on our streets, countless people left homeless by hurricanes, earthquakes, fires, and tsunamis), take away the multiplied images of brutality that accost us on the TV news programs we watch and in the movies we choose to see, and we are left with the staggering blunt force of personal misery. How far we have fallen from the unspoiled freshness and peaceful security of our original Eden home!

In his book *Theology of Culture,* Paul Tillich refers to Picasso's *Guernica* as "a great Protestant painting." Tillich explains, "The Protestant principle emphasizes the infinite distance between God and man." Then he rejoices in the breathtaking theological truth that bridges that gulf: "It is man in anxiety, guilt, and despair who is the object of God's unconditional acceptance."[2]

---

1. For more on Picasso and his protests against war in his art, see Sidra Stich, "Picasso's Art and Politics in 1936," *Arts Magazine,* October 1983, vol. 58, pp. 113–118; *Picasso's Guernica,* ed. Ellen C. Oppler (New York: W.W. Norton, Norton Critical Studies in Art History, 1988); and Herschel B. Chipp, *Picasso's Guernica: History, Transformations, Meanings* (Berkeley: University of California Press, 1988).

2. Paul Tillich, *Theology of Culture* (London: Oxford University Press, 1959), 68.

Troubled by Their Times

Has the end-time topic of the time of trouble ever been presented to you in a way that left you frightened? Do you look forward to that time just before Jesus returns or have you found yourself dreading it? Do you think God gave us the information to scare us into being good?

I used to know so much about the time of trouble.

Before I had graduated from elementary school, my views were very clearly formed about those traumatic days just before Jesus returns the second time. I remember a few of the people who taught me. There was a serious Sabbath School leader, a pastor who repeated warnings from the Bible, an evangelist who notified us of the precipitous time in which we lived, my stern seventh- and eighth-grade teacher who tested us on the topic, a visiting former nun who graphically described to our church what was about to happen to us, and a few church members who seldom spoke of any other subject.

These end-time enthusiasts in the little church of my childhood already knew where they were going to hide when it came time to "run to the hills." Some of them had buried canned food and water, blankets and other supplies, to ensure their survival. They scanned the newspaper every morning for news of legislation aimed at forcing Sabbath keepers to abandon the fourth commandment. They were cautious of making too much show about their religion, about talking too much when they went to the grocery store or when they picked up their prophetic publications from the post office. "You know what happened to the Waldenses," they would admonish, and then they'd tell me stories of those medieval Protestants living in constant fear in caves in Italy while Roman troops stalked the mountain hideaways looking for fugitives.

The evangelist informed us that false christs might soon arrive in spaceships that would land near Palm Springs in the southern California desert at a place where he said he had secretly witnessed the preparations being made. The former nun told us that in the basement of every local Catholic church there was a concealed room that already had instruments of torture ready to force us to recant. The Sabbath School leader, it seemed to me, incorporated Matthew 24 into every lesson: "Watch out . . . ," "handed over . . . ," "persecution . . . ," "put to death . . . ," "dreadful . . . ," "betrayal . . . ," "great distress . . ." The pastor recommended that we read *Foxe's Book of Martyrs.* To this day, I have difficulty dislodging the deeply embedded fear they instilled.

I remember three distinctive features of those early apocalyptic warnings. The first was the sheer intensity of every discussion about the last days. I thought I could feel my heart rate accelerating and my blood pressure rising. Sometimes I had a hard time getting to sleep at night. I remember walking home from school one day and suddenly realizing I was at the corner of the church that had "the concealed torture room." I sped up, crossed to the other side of the street, and walked by quickly, not daring to turn around to see whether someone was following me.

I was careful not to tell anybody how afraid I was of heights to be sure that information didn't fall into the hands of some devious traitor who would help capture me one dark night, take me to an unfenced tower, and use my fear to make me talk. I worried about whether I could live through such demanding times. Would I be strong enough? Or loyal enough? Or would I collapse under the pressure, betray my mother and my sisters, and denounce the Sabbath?

I can't begin to tell you of all the people who have shared similar experiences

> "This is what the LORD says:
> 'Maintain justice
>   and do what is right,
> for my salvation is close at hand
>   and my righteousness will soon be
>   revealed' " (Isaiah 56:1).
>
> "The revelation of Jesus Christ, which God gave him to show his servants what must soon take place" (Revelation 1:1).
>
> "I am coming soon. Hold on to what you have, so that no one will take your crown" (3:11).
>
> "Behold, I am coming soon!" (22:12).

with me. They've told me of their nightmares, their anxieties, and their lingering fears. People have told me that they've actually hoped that Jesus wouldn't come back in their lifetimes because they're convinced they wouldn't be able to survive the ordeal. People have confessed to me a riveting, consuming fascination with the time of trouble that somehow eclipses the much more rewarding study of Jesus, who promises to cut those days short and rescue us (Matthew 24:22; 1 Thessalonians 1:10). What have we done to Christ's counsel, "Do not let your hearts be troubled" (John 14:1)?

The second feature of the end-time messages I received dealt with when the time of trouble would take place. Above all, I learned that it was going to be soon! "Keep watch," Jesus told us, "because you do not know on what day your Lord will come" (24:42). Like a thief in the night. When you least expect it. As it was in the days of Noah.

I'll admit it: I was confused by the biblical concept of soon. I asked my teacher how an earthquake in Portugal in 1755 or a meteorite shower in 1833 could indicate soon. She replied that it had been prophesied, it had been fulfilled, and that was that! "With the Lord a day is like a thousand years, and a thousand years are like a day" (2 Peter 3:8). End of discussion. No more questions.

The third clear instruction I received about the end times was that whenever that soon happened, it would happen ini-tially in the United States of America. The persecution of early Christians is not a matter of prophetic fulfillment, I was taught, but one of church history. Oppression of European Waldenses doesn't qualify. The Holocaust happened to Jews, so it doesn't meet the specifications either. Neither does the treatment of Russians or Cambodians or even the Christians of India, Iraq, or southern Sudan. The "time of trouble" is not just a time of trouble, the instruction proclaimed, it has to follow certain legislative and political events in the specific order, at the fixed time, and in the proper place.

Along with many of my friends, I felt the pull of last-day subjects during college. After political science classes, we would stay in the classroom and discuss how American Adventists could best prepare for the end time. We became conversant in religious liberty issues and court cases. We talked about becoming attorneys so we could defend Sabbatarians, perhaps all the way to America's Supreme Court. We examined the records of political candidates closely, searching their voting patterns for clues to their position on the separation of church and state. Should we even put our hand over our heart and swear allegiance to the United States of America, we wondered, if one day the government was going to turn on its citizens, pass laws that would force us to obey against our religious convictions, threaten us with imprisonment if we refused to obey, and even pass a capital punishment statute against dissidents?

Intensity. Immediacy. American. Put them all together, and they spelled fear for me. The dreadful time of trouble, just around the corner in time and place, demanded our attention, crowded out other spiritual considerations, and undercut any assurance we felt about who would save us.

DID JESUS INTEND TO FRIGHTEN US?

Today, I don't know as much about the time of trouble as I did when I was in elementary school. But there are a few things I know for sure. I'm certain that when Jesus told us about the end times, He didn't do it to frighten us. Fear, it turns out, is a lousy motivator. It might momentarily turn us in a different direction. But it doesn't last long, and it ends up producing negative behavior. In a restaurant, recently, I saw a mother get up, walk around the table, and squeeze her little daughter's face until it puckered. "If you don't eat this food right now," the mother threatened loudly enough for all

of us to hear, "I'll blister you when we get home." The child quickly ate two bites—and then quit eating again.

Family specialists tell us that

while a parent may be able to scare a child into immediate behavior changes with a threat or using fear, in the long term it can be bad for the child and very hard on the parent-child relationship. . . . Whether it is a young child who is being threatened to be left behind in the grocery store because she won't keep up, or threatening violence or other hurtful things in order to get the child to do what we want, it is manipulative behavior on the parent's part and using fear as a motivator will eventually backfire. . . . If a child thinks that the parent will give him away or hurt him if he does not do what the parent wants, what sort of unconditional love or security is being provided? How will the child experience the security and trust that he needs as a balance to all those other scary things that are going on in the world outside the family?[1]

"The LORD is a refuge for the oppressed,
   a stronghold in times of trouble"
      (Psalm 9:9).

"In the day of trouble
   he will keep me safe in his dwelling;
he will hide me in the shelter of his
      tabernacle
   and set me high upon a rock"
      (Psalm 27: 5).

"The salvation of the righteous
      comes from the LORD;
   he is their stronghold in time of
      trouble" (Psalm 37:39).

"Praise be to the God and Father of our
Lord Jesus Christ, the Father of compassion
and the God of all comfort, who comforts us
in all our troubles" (2 Corinthians 1:3, 4).

Business management research tells us the same thing: "In the short-term one may be able to squeeze out more production using fear as a motivator, but in the long-term it is very problematic."[2]

Don't you agree that our heavenly Parent understands motivational principles even better than we do? Are we really to believe that the One who told us not to let our hearts be troubled and that it would be much better for us to trust in Him (John 14:1) suddenly changed His mind and now thinks that it would be preferable if we were a whole lot more worried and afraid?

God isn't the one who tries to scare us into His embrace; He's the One we turn to when we're unsettled. "I am troubled; O Lord, come to my aid" (Isaiah 38:14). He is our Refuge in times of trouble, our safe Dwelling Place, our Stronghold, and our Source of comfort. "Peace I leave with you," Jesus assures us. "Do not let your hearts be troubled and do not be afraid" (John 14:27).

But what about those Matthew 24 warnings: "Flee to the mountains . . ." "How dreadful it will be in those days . . ." "Great distress unequalled since the beginning of the world until now . . ."? And don't forget all the "fear God" verses. "Fear God and keep his commandments" (Ecclesiastes 12:13). "Fear God and give him glory" (Revelation 14:7). Maybe we should be afraid!

I'm sure you've heard it said over and over again that the biblical phrase "fear God" means to "honor" or "respect" Him (see the Contemporary English Version of Ecclesiastes 12:13, for example). *The Seventh-day Adventist Bible Commentary* insists that the word is not used "in the sense of being afraid of God, but in the sense of coming to Him with reverence and awe." "To 'fear' God," the *Commentary* says, "is to regard Him with profound and reverent respect and to have proper regard for His will."[3]

> RHYTHMIC PARALLELISM:
>
> "The heavens declare the glory of God;
>   the skies proclaim the work of
>   his hands" (Psalm 19:1).
>
> "God is our refuge and strength,
>   an ever-present help in trouble"
>   (Psalm 46:1).
>
> INTERPRETIVE PARALLELISM:
>
> "Who is a God like you?
>   Who pardons sin and forgives the
>   transgression of the remnant of
>   his inheritance" (Micah 7:18).
>
> "You have heard that it was said, 'Love your neighbor and hate your enemy.' But I tell you: Love your enemies, pray for those who persecute you" (Matthew 5:43, 44).

However, there's something more here too—something bigger than just a change in our understanding of the word. Bible scholars long have recognized that the fundamental meaning of a biblical passage is often most clearly revealed, not by the definitions of the words themselves, but by the literary structure of the passage. The underlying structure of biblical verse is parallelism, a technique that has to do with the symmetry of clauses within a passage.[4] This literary method operates in two ways. In rhythmic parallelism, the second line of a couplet uses different words to repeat the content of the first line. In interpretive parallelism, the second line enlarges upon and further explains the first line.

The case can easily be made that the psalmist used this structure to help us understand "the fear of God." The Bible maintains that "there is no fear in love"; that, in fact, "perfect love drives out fear" (1 John 4:18). By the principle of interpretive parallelism, then, the perfect love of God toward us will drive fear from us, not instill fear in us. And by the same principle, the more perfect our love for God, the less we will fear Him.

Do you see in the structure of the following psalms the insight that fearing God means more than just respecting Him; it means focusing on His unfailing, enduring love?

> The eyes of the LORD are on those
>   who fear him,
>   on those whose hope is
>   in his unfailing love
>   (Psalm 33:18).

The LORD delights in those who
    fear him,
who put their hope in his
    unfailing love (Psalm
    147:11).

Let those who fear the LORD say:
    "His love endures forever"
    (Psalm 118:4).

The parallelism of these psalms helps us to better understand what the Bible wants us to know about the fear of God. Biblical fear of God means trusting God for deliverance, forgiveness, and redemption. Fearing God means relying fully on God's mercy. It means recognizing that God blots out our sin. It means glorifying God and singing His praise for doing for us what we can't do for ourselves. It means claiming His promise of salvation. It means placing our hope for eternal life in His grace alone.

So when the three angels' messages ask us to "fear God and give Him glory," we are hearing the proclamation of the everlasting gospel, the loud declaration that salvation is only from God, never from what we do or contribute. That's the message that brings persecution and trouble.

Paul invites Timothy not to be afraid to join him in his suffering because of the

"Give thanks to the LORD,
    for he is good; his love endures forever.
Cry out, 'Save us, O God our Savior;
    gather us and deliver us from the
    nations,
that we may give thanks to your holy
    name,
    that we may glory in your praise' "
    (1 Chronicles 16:34).

"Have mercy on me, O God,
    according to your unfailing love;
according to your great compassion
    blot out my transgressions"
    (Psalm 51:1).

"In your unfailing love you will lead
    the people you have redeemed"
    (Exodus 15:13).

"I trust in your unfailing love;
    my heart rejoices in your salvation"
    (Psalm 13:5).

"May your unfailing love come to me, O
    LORD,
your salvation according to your
    promise" (Psalm 119:41).

"Put your hope in the LORD,
    for with the LORD is unfailing love
    and with him is full redemption"
    (Psalm 130:7).

gospel. Notice his words of encouragement and conviction to his youthful friend:

Do not be ashamed to testify

about our Lord, or ashamed of me his prisoner. But join with me in suffering for the gospel, by the power of God, who has saved us and called us to a holy life—not because of anything we have done but because of his own purpose and grace. This grace was given us in Christ Jesus before the beginning of time, but it has now been revealed through the appearing of our Savior, Christ Jesus, who has destroyed death and has brought life and immortality to light through the gospel. And of this gospel I was appointed a herald and an apostle and a teacher. That is why I am suffering as I am. Yet I am not ashamed, because I know whom I have believed, and am convinced that he is able to guard what I have entrusted to him for that day (2 Timothy 1:8–12).

In advance of the time of trouble,

"make up your mind not to worry beforehand how you will defend yourselves. For I will give you words and wisdom that none of your adversaries will be able to resist or contradict. . . .

"When these things begin to take place, stand up and lift up your heads, because your redemption is drawing near" (Luke 21:14, 15, 28).

Knowing about the time of trouble is not supposed to frighten us. It builds our confidence in the God who delivers us. It convinces us that He is able. It encourages us to trust in His unfailing love and His promise of salvation. And it inspires us to give to God our fears about that time.

Yes, Jesus does speak of "great distress, unequaled from the beginning of the world until now" (Matthew 24:21). But certainly He wasn't meaning to minimize or make light of what people already had endured in His name—and no one's mental anguish or physical suffering is greater than anyone else's when it is of the same intensity and duration. Perhaps Jesus wanted us to expect broader persecution, unequaled in geographic scope, occurring in many places at the same time. Or perhaps there is an unequaled tenacity to the persecutors at the end of time, one that brings into even sharper relief the differences between our weakness and God's strength. We don't know. What we are certain of is that knowing about the time of trouble doesn't terrorize us. It builds our confidence in the God who delivers us. It convinces us that He is able. It encourages us to trust in His unfailing love and His promise of salvation. And it inspires us to give to God our fears about that time.

HOW SOON IS SOON?

What about the "soon-ness" of the time of trouble? Should that be worrisome to us?

The disciples also wanted to know. "When will this happen?" they ask Jesus, "and what will be the sign of your coming and of the end of the age?" (Matthew 24:3). Jesus answers their questions and promises that those days will be shortened "for the sake of the elect, whom he has chosen" (Mark 13:20), and then, to build their confidence, He says, "See, I have told you ahead of time" (Matthew 24:25). "When you hear of wars and revolutions, do not be frightened. These things must happen first, but the end will not come right away" (Luke 21:9). The gospel "will be preached in the whole world" (Matthew 24:14), the "distress of those days" will take place (24:29), and then "the Son of Man will appear in the sky" (24:30). The sequence is established. The prophecies begin to be fulfilled. The signs of the last days appear. "When you see these things happening, you know that it is near, right at the door" (Mark 13:29).

Nevertheless, people continue to arrive on the scene and then pass away without seeing the end. My grandmother often told me that she was convinced the Second Coming would happen in her lifetime. She died in the late 1960s. My mother assured me that Jesus would return before she reached the end of her life. She succumbed to cancer in 1987. In high school, Karen and I were pretty certain the world would end before we got to college. Now we think about the days when our second- and third-grade grandchildren will go to college. Hasn't the likelihood of a soon Second Coming completely lost its plausibility?

The problem is that so many of us misplace our interest in being authentic *end-time people* and instead become frantic *timing-of-the-end people.* Our focus shifts so easily from what God has done and is doing in our lives to what will happen next in the prophetic sequence. Rather than concentrate on God's whisperings to us today—"if anyone hears my voice and opens the door, I will come in" (Revelation 3:20)—we exhibit a preference for listening for the next loud announcement of the end. When our Bible studies and evangelistic sermons emphasize the trumpets rather than the invitations of God, when we shout the warnings so loudly that people have a difficult time hearing the whisperings, we shift the focus away from welcoming Jesus into our lives right now.

And then we really get ourselves into trouble! In establishing the timing of the end as the cornerstone of our faith, we tend to forget the fragile, temporary nature of life on planet Earth in the present. We forget that our claim on robust health is at best tenuous; we just don't have any guarantees that we'll be alive next week, to say nothing of lasting all the way to the Second Coming. Every time I get on an airplane, I realize the possible danger. Every time we venture onto southern California freeways, we understand the risk. But it doesn't require a big or dramatic disaster. A friend of ours was hit and killed by a car while he was walking on a quiet sidewalk. A church member was gunned down in a robbery while she was innocently depositing the previous Sabbath's church offering in the bank. Another friend collapsed and died while he was hiking in the mountains. Karen's mother died after choking on her food during a meal.

For each of those dear people, and for millions just like them every year all around the world, soon comes much sooner than they expect. The younger you are, the more difficult it is to accept such a possibility— but soon happens anyway. For the great majority of all the people who have ever lived on earth, there is no time of trouble and there are no signs of the end: no dark days, no falling stars, no last plagues, no legislation, no persecution, and no celestial Rider on a white horse. For these people, the end came unexpectedly, without warning, like a thief in the night. Soon!

The immediacy of the time of trouble

> "Who shall separate us from the love of Christ? Shall trouble or hardship or persecution or famine or nakedness or danger or sword? As it is written:
>
> 'For your sake we face death all day long;
> we are considered as sheep to be slaughtered.'
>
> No, in all these things we are more than conquerors through him who loved us. For I am convinced that neither death nor life, neither angels nor demons, neither the present nor the future, nor any powers, neither height nor depth, nor anything else in all creation, will be able to separate us from the love of God that is in Christ Jesus our Lord" (Romans 8:35–39).

is not supposed to frighten us. The end of history on our planet will occur soon enough, without being hastened along to its conclusion by any worrying on our part. Our short lifespan should only persuade us to confidently establish the priorities of Christ-centered living today and to celebrate finding the fullness of joy in His presence right now (Psalm 16:11). "It is good to wait quietly / for the salvation of the LORD," whose "compassions never fail. / They are new every morning" (Lamentations 3:26, 22, 23). Give me the freshness of God's grace any day—the time of trouble will take care of itself! "Morning by morning he dispenses his justice, / and every new day he does not fail" (Zephaniah 3:5).

AN AMERICAN TIME OF TROUBLE?

The Smithsonian's National Museum of American History in Washington, D.C., has on display the fifteen-star, fifteen-stripe flag that was raised during the defense of Fort McHenry in Baltimore Harbor on the night of September 13, 1814. This was the flag that inspired Francis Scott Key to write the words to what became America's national anthem, "The Star-Spangled Banner."

A half-century after the song was writ-

ten, the first shots of the American Civil War were fired at Fort Sumter in Charleston Harbor, South Carolina. Federal soldiers were forced to surrender, and the Southern army, according to some reports, played "The Star-Spangled Banner" as they raised the Confederate flag over the fort. Indignant about the use of the anthem under those circumstances, Oliver Wendell Holmes wrote a fifth stanza for the song. It begins:

"When our land is illumined by
    liberty's smile,
If a foe from within strikes a blow
    at her glory,
Down, down with the traitor that
    tries to defile
The flag of the stars, and the page
    of her story!"

In the turbulent days between the bombardment of Fort McHenry and the attack on Fort Sumter, the Seventh-day Adventist Church was born in America. At the time, another maelstrom was raging—a theological one that focused people's attention on dramatic predictions of the end of the world. As the young leaders of the new church searched their Bibles for understanding, their conviction grew that the charge of being "a foe from within" once again would be leveled in America. And this time, "the traitor that tries to defile" would be American citizens committed to honoring the seventh-day Sabbath in spite of the fact that a different Sabbath had become the law of the land.

As America grew into a superpower, the church in North America also grew. Although it sent missionaries to other parts of the world (beginning officially in 1874 when J. N. Andrews left the United States and began working in Switzerland), the membership of the Adventist Church remained primarily American for decades. The steady tithe base, the generous giving in support of missions, the doctrinal foundations, the publishing endeavors, and the administrative leadership all continued to be principally American.

Today, it's a different story. With churches established in more than two hundred countries around the globe, the North American membership represents only about 6 percent of the total church membership, which is in excess of fifteen million. Along with international growth, our perspective has broadened to include sisters and brothers from countries we struggle to locate on a world map. While our prophetic expectations remain grounded in the "sure word" of God (2 Peter 1:19, KJV), we no longer can interpret the end-time

prophecies exclusively from an American point of view.

In countries all around the world today, belonging to a religious minority is a crime.[5] Freedom of religion is severely limited. Evangelism is prohibited. Christian-owned buildings have been appropriated by the civil authorities. In many Muslim-dominated countries, there is open discrimination against non-Muslims and particularly against Christians.[6]

Police in Uzbekistan and Azerbaijan, without any governmental restraint, harass members of religious minorities, interrupt church services, and arrest pastors. In the islands of Comoros, where Roman Catholics are the main Christian minority, most Christians do not openly practice their faith for fear of discrimination. Citizens who convert to Christianity are treated more cruelly than foreigners who practice their faith.

In April 2007, in Eritrea, eighty members of an Evangelical Presbyterian church were arrested after Sunday worship services. In September of that year, Eritrean authorities tortured a woman to death for refusing to recant her Christian faith. Ten Christian women were arrested at another church meeting and spent eighteen months in jail "under severe pressure." The government has singled out Jehovah's

Witnesses for the harshest treatment. They are denied passports and identity cards, their marriages cannot be legalized, and they can be imprisoned without charges.

The military regime in Myanmar (formerly Burma) regulates and restricts the expression of religion and speech and infiltrates religious groups to spy on their activities. Buddhist monks march peacefully against government policy toward minorities, including Muslim groups, who, because of their faith, have been evicted from their homes and forced to live in refugee camps. The government has used deadly force to suppress dissent.

In the Democratic Peoples Republic of Korea, there is a strict ban on foreign missionaries and all forms of proselytizing. Turkish television regularly broadcasts anti-Christian messages. The nation of Bhutan restricts the practice of non-Buddhist religions; it is a crime to challenge anyone's belief or culture through written or verbal communication. In Ethiopia, discrimination against Ethiopian Jews is widespread. In Lebanon, every identification card must identify the person's religious affiliation. In Afghanistan, the Sunni majority discriminates against all other religions, including other branches of Islam. In Iran, pastors caught evangelizing Muslims have been hanged.

The time of trouble isn't waiting for America. It's taking place today, right now, while you're reading this paragraph, in many places in the world! And it's happening against people of all faiths—Jews, Buddhists, and Muslims—and against all stripes of Christians—Sabbath keepers included, but certainly not limited to them.

God's end-time people are troubled by the times in which they live. They are passionate about freedom and vigilant in the defense of liberty. They see religious intolerance in all its forms as the fury of our enemy, the great dragon, "that ancient serpent called the devil, or Satan," set into motion "because he knows that his time is short" (Revelation 12:9, 12). They understand that discrimination of any kind against anyone anywhere in the world prepares the way for discrimination against all of us wherever we live, no matter what our color or culture or creed or orientation.

When a Buddhist student is singled out for harsh treatment in her school because she is Buddhist, end-time students stand with her. When Muslim families are driven from their homes and relocated in refugee camps because they are Muslim, end-time families take exception. When Jewish synagogues are vandalized and covered with hate messages because the worshipers are Jews, end-time worshipers volunteer to help clean up and put pressure on the legal systems that don't fully prosecute such outrages.

When Presbyterians and Jehovah's Witnesses and Roman Catholics are jailed and beaten and executed because their religion is different from the majority, end-time people of faith defend them and provide for their grieving families. When Sabbath-keeping teens in non-Christian countries cannot complete the tests necessary to stay in school because of their belief, end-time people around the world protest.

When agnostics and atheists are compelled by Christian nations to honor the Ten Commandments or pledge their allegiance to a country "under God" before they can be "full citizens," end-time people find ways to safeguard their sensibilities.

All of us are created with the inalienable right to hold to our faith as we see it or to choose to hold to no faith at all. End-time people are troubled by each instance in which that power of choice is restricted.

End-time people understand the intimidating severity of the last days of trouble. But they aren't paralyzed by fear. They aren't waiting for signs to appear before they establish a relationship with Jesus.

They aren't deferring their response to God until something more or something else takes place. They know that Jesus warned that the stress of the time of the end will make people indifferent to the sufferings of others, that "the love of most will grow cold" (Matthew 24:12). But they are learning to loathe indifference; they want their love to stay warm *right now.*

So, *today,* end-time people are looking for ways to reveal the never-failing compassion of the God who promises to love us and be with us all the way "to the very end of the age" (Matthew 28:20). *Today,* end-time people are striving to exemplify the full inclusivity of Jesus to our world: "Here there is no Greek or Jew, circumcised or uncircumcised, barbarian, Scythian, slave or free, but Christ is all, and is in all" (Colossians 3:11). *Now, in the present,* end-time people are proclaiming, "where the Spirit of the Lord is there is freedom" (2 Corinthians 3:17).

"The Spirit of the Sovereign LORD is on me," end-time people repeat Isaiah's words with Jesus, as they join Jesus in ministry *now.*

> The LORD has anointed me to
> preach good news to the poor.
> He has sent me to bind up the
> brokenhearted,

to proclaim freedom for the
captives
and release from darkness for
the prisoners (Isaiah 61:1;
compare Luke 4:18).

"Even *now*," declares the LORD,
"return to me with all your
hearts." . . .
Be not afraid, O land;
be glad and rejoice.
Surely the LORD has done great
things (Joel 2:12, 21).

"Do not be afraid, little flock, for your Father has been pleased to give you the kingdom" (Luke 12:32).

---

1. Kori Rodley Irons, Families.com/26 March 2008.

2. W. Cron, J. Slocum, D. VandeWalle, and Q. Fu, "Encountering Setbacks, Setting Goals and the Role of Goal Orientation," *Human Performance* 18 (2005) 55–80.

3. *The Seventh-day Adventist Bible Commentary,* F. D. Nichol, ed. (Washington, D.C.: Review and Herald®, 1953, 1957), 7:827 (on Revelation 14:7); and 1:968 (on Deuteronomy 4:10).

4. "Like the swing of a pendulum to and fro," Richard Moulton wrote over a hundred years ago, "the versification of the Bible moves with a rhythm of parallel lines." Richard Moulton, *The Literary Study of the Bible* (Boston, Mass.: D. C. Heath & Co., 1899), 47.

5. For more statistics and reports of religious discrimination, see the *Religious Freedom World Report, 2006–2007,* published by the Public Affairs and Religious Liberty Department of the General Conference of Seventh-day Adventists, Silver Spring, Maryland, and the International Religious Liberty Institute of Andrews University, Berrien Springs, Michigan. The reports in this chapter are mostly taken from that publication.

6. Bangladesh is 83 percent Muslim. Jordan's population is 92 percent Sunni Muslim. Somalia is 99.9 percent Muslim. Among the three-million-plus citizens of Mauritania, there are, according to one report, just seven Adventists.

VISION NUMBER SIX
DANIEL 7:9–14

"As I looked,
"thrones were set in place,
    and the Ancient of Days took his seat.
His clothing was as white as snow;
    the hair of his head was white like wool.
His throne was flaming with fire,
    and its wheels were all ablaze.
A river of fire was flowing,
    coming out from before him.
Thousands upon thousands attended him;
    ten thousand times ten thousand stood before him.
The court was seated, and the books were opened.

"Then I continued to watch because of the boastful words the horn was speaking. I kept looking until the beast was slain and its body destroyed and thrown into the blazing fire. (The other beasts had been stripped of their authority, but were allowed to live for a period of time.)

"In my vision at night I looked, and there before me was one like a son of man, coming with the clouds of heaven. He approached the Ancient of Days and was led into his presence. He was given authority, glory and sovereign power; all peoples, nations and men of every language worshiped him. His dominion is an everlasting dominion that will not pass away, and his kingdom is one that will never be destroyed."

THE TERRIFYING NATURE OF THE SACRIFICE

*If you were to create a monument to the Christian experience,
what would you commemorate? Would you focus on an act of
overcoming? A moment of triumphal obedience? Or would you
memorialize the Christian's great need?*

King Edward III had just led England to a decisive victory against France in the Battle of Crécy. Now Edward turns his attention to the town of Calais, a significant French port on the English Channel. In September 1346, the English army lays siege to Calais, hoping the citizens of Calais will weaken quickly and surrender. But the French are more determined and resilient than the English had anticipated, and eleven months later, the siege is still underway.

Inside Calais, however, the people are suffering. Their provisions of food have been exhausted. Their water supply has dried up. Their hopes to outlast the siege have come to an end. Summoning an emissary from the king of England, the mayor of Calais pleads for mercy and requests the English to allow the surviving citizens of Calais to leave their city, abandoning it to Edward.

Sir Walter Manny, the English emissary, replies that Edward is so angry about their obstinate defense that had cost the English so many lives and so much money that he insists on unconditional surrender. The mayor of Calais asks again for mercy, and the emissary returns to the English camp.

Edward listens to the pleas of the mayor, scoffs, and sends Sir Walter back with a refinement of his demand. If six of the principal citizens of Calais will march out of town with bare heads and feet, with ropes around their necks, and with the keys to the town in their hands, he will execute the six but spare the rest of the town.

When the people of Calais, summoned to the town hall by the ringing of a bell, hear the conditions, they react with horror and discouragement. After all they have endured, now the English king demands a further sacrifice. Who among them would agree to give himself up? We are told that even the mayor wept bitterly.

After a momentary pause, the wealthiest merchant in Calais, Eustache de Saint-Pierre, stands up and volunteers: "I name myself as the first of the six." Another man, rich and respected, joins his friend. Then another and another step forward. In just a moment, there are six volunteers willing to sacrifice themselves for the survival of the rest of the town.

The six volunteers from Calais are led into the presence of the English king, and they fall to their knees before him. They are a pitiful sight. Emaciated. Dressed in what is basically their underwear. Nooses around their necks. Emotionally beaten. They plead for mercy. But the king remains unmoved and orders them to be beheaded.

English barons ask their king not to act so cruelly. They plead with him to spare these honorable citizens. Then the queen, Phillipa, steps forward. About to deliver Edward's child, she kneels before him. "I have never asked you one favor. Now, I most humbly ask as a gift, for the sake of the Son of the blessed Mary and for your love to me, that you will be merciful to these six men."

Edward stares in silence at Phillipa. Finally, he says to her, "I cannot refuse you. I give them to you to do as you please."

The queen moves quickly. She takes the six volunteers to her apartments, has the nooses taken from around their necks, gives them new clothes, and feeds them. Then she asks six English nobles to escort them back to Calais as heroes. The English lift the siege and go home. Calais survives.

Five long centuries pass.

The French again suffer devastating military defeats, this time in the Franco-Prussian

Auguste Rodin, *The Burghers of Calais*
To view this sculpture in color, go to www.pacificpress.com/chosenbygrace.

war. French politicians realize that it would be good to recognize the patriotic sacrifices their young soldiers have made for their country. Early in the 1880s, the new mayor of Calais proposes one such recognition: a monumental sculpture to the fourteenth-century heroes who saved his city—the leading citizens, or *burghers,* of Calais.

The municipal council of Calais chooses Auguste Rodin to be their sculptor. Already renowned in France, the innovative Rodin is a brilliant choice to do the work, and it is a tribute to the city of Calais that he accepts the commission. However, by 1885, there is trouble. The council had envisioned an elegant tribute to the actions of their brave hero, Eustache de Saint-Pierre, who had confidently rescued Calais from Edward III. Contrary to these desires, Rodin chooses to show all six burghers *in the moment of surrender.* Dressed in their "shirts and breeches," vulnerable and conflicted, with heads bowed and eyes downcast, one holding his head in his hands, the sculpture depicts people who are convinced they are marching to their execution. Rodin's burghers are frail, humble, hesitant, and defeated.

The great sculptor explains: "They are still questioning themselves to know if they have the strength to accomplish the supreme sacrifice—their soul pushes them onward, but their feet refuse to walk. They drag themselves along painfully, as much because of the feebleness to which famine has reduced them as because of the terrifying nature of the sacrifice."

Weeks of argument ensue. The council insists on having its way. Rodin refuses, saying that the council's limited and formulaic vision would produce a work that was "cold, static and conventional." The council complains that Rodin's depiction of "defeated postures offended our religion." They demand a modification. Rodin dismisses the criticism. He writes to the mayor of Calais, stating flatly that the council's demands would "emasculate" his work.

The council holds to its reservations but ultimately agrees to allow Rodin to finish the monument. On June 3, 1895, *The Burghers of Calais* is at last unveiled in the Richelieu Garden in Calais.

Today, the power of the sculpture is universally recognized and lauded. The original statue remains in Calais, with additional casts in London, Paris, Copenhagen, Jerusalem, Seoul, Tokyo, Canberra, Washington, D.C., Pasadena, Booklyn, and Manhattan.

Rodin's determined insight proves to be profound, especially to end-time Christians. We become victorious when we confess our weaknesses, not when we trumpet our strengths.[1]

---

1. For the story and quotations, I've depended on Nelly Silagy Benedek, *Auguste Rodin—The Burghers of Calais: A Resource for Educators* (New York City: The Metropolitan Museum of Art, 2000).

Chapter Six
Tested by the Sabbath

Why should we listen to God? Does He speak to us with purpose? Do His words lead us somewhere important? Is it possible to discern His purpose? Is there something we can do to keep returning to that purpose?

Who is GOD that I should listen to him?" (Exodus 5:2, *The Message*).

An ancient Egyptian Pharaoh, unaccustomed to being told what to do, rises from his throne, looks directly into the eyes of Moses and Aaron, and asks the question. And frankly, it's a good question. A question we all need to ask. "Why should we listen?"

Initially, the elders of the Israelites listened to the answer given by Moses and Aaron. They observed the miraculous signs performed by the brothers (4:1–9). The staff-to-snake-to-staff demonstration caught their attention. The leprous hand restored was impressive. By the time the jar of water from the Nile was turned to blood, they were true believers (4:29–31). What really touched them, however, was the welcome news that God is concerned about their situation. "They bowed down and worshiped" (4:31).

But that was a few days ago.

Since then, Moses' request for three days off so the Israelites could journey into the desert for a "festival" is rejected outright. The Pharaoh orders them back to work under even harsher circumstances. Their foremen are beaten severely as a cruel warning of what might happen to all of them (5:1–18). Suddenly, the staff-to-snake-to-staff thing doesn't matter so much.

The battered foremen find Moses and Aaron. All the talk about miracles and festivals and worship is over. " 'You have made us a stench to Pharaoh and his officials,' " the foremen accuse, " 'and have put a sword in their hand to kill us' " (5:21). Leave us alone! We'd rather be slaves making bricks than follow you out into the desert to worship a god we don't know. Why should we listen to you or to God?

Now it's Moses' turn to complain. "Why have you brought trouble upon this people?" Moses asks the God of the burning bush. "Is this why you sent me? Ever since I went to Pharaoh to speak in your name, he has brought trouble upon this people, and you have not rescued your people at all" (5:22, 23).

Who is God that I should listen to Him? What has He done for me lately?

Listen to how God answers the question.

> "I have heard the groaning of the Israelites, whom the Egyptians are enslaving, and I have remembered my covenant.
>
> "Therefore, say to the Israel-

ites: 'I am the LORD, and I will bring you out from under the yoke of the Egyptians. I will free you from being slaves to them, and I will redeem you with an outstretched arm and with mighty acts of judgment. I will take you as my own people, and I will be your God. Then you will know that I am the LORD your God, who brought you out from under the yoke of the Egyptians. And I will bring you to the land I swore with uplifted hand to give to Abraham, to Isaac and to Jacob. I will give it to you as a possession. I am the LORD'" (6:5–8).

"I have heard." "I have remembered." "I will bring you out." "I will free you." "I will redeem you." "I will take you as my own people." "I will be your God." "I will bring you to the land." "I will give it to you."

Who is this God? Why should we listen to Him? Because He is the One intimately involved in our daily lives (Psalm 23). He knows where we live (Revelation 2:13). He doesn't leave us to ourselves, even in our most trying circumstances (Romans 8:38, 39). He knows what we need before we ask for help (Matthew 6:8). Because He gives only those gifts He knows will

> "Was it because there were no graves in Egypt that you brought us to the desert to die?" (Exodus 14:11).
>
> "If only we had died by the LORD's hand in Egypt! . . . You have brought us out into this desert to starve . . . to death" (16:3).
>
> "Why did you bring us up out of Egypt to make us and our children and livestock die of thirst?" (17:3).

> "They did not keep God's covenant
>   and refused to live by his law.
> They forgot what he had done,
>   the wonders he had shown them"
>   (Psalm 78:10, 11).
>
> "They continued to sin against him,
>   rebelling in the desert against the
>   Most High.
> They willfully put God to the test"
>   (78:17, 18).
>
> "They did not believe in God
>   or trust in his deliverance" (78:22).
>
> "Because of your great compassion you did not abandon them in the desert. By day the pillar of cloud did not cease to guide them on their path, nor the pillar of fire by night to shine on the way they were to take. You gave your good Spirit to instruct them. You did not withhold your manna from their mouths, and you gave them water for their thirst. For forty years you sustained them in the desert; they lacked nothing, their clothes did not wear out nor did their feet become swollen" (Nehemiah 9:19–21).

Moses is leading the Israelites farther and farther away from the land of their bondage. But the people whine like they did in Egypt. They grumble and wish out loud that they had never left the land of their captivity.

In such a short time, the triumphant songs of Moses and Miriam have faded as the Israelites forget that God hurled Pharaoh's chariots and his army into the Red Sea (Exodus 15:4). The bitter waters of Marah that God turned sweet and the twelve springs and seventy palm trees of Elim to which God led them aren't enough to keep their thoughts on their majestic God, "awesome in glory, working wonders" (15:11). The brutality of their slavery in Egypt has somehow been transformed in their porous memories into a pleasant existence beside the Nile, where "we sat around pots of meat and ate all the food we wanted" (16:3). They lose their focus on what God has done in their behalf and turn their attention to what they are doing and not doing and to the circumstances and forces that are bent on thwarting God's purposes for them.

God needs to step in to try to restore the proper focus.

That's exactly what He does. He tells Moses just what is needed to make this refocusing happen among His redeemed

ultimately make us happy (Ecclesiastes 5:19). Because He has promised, and He always keeps His promises (Hebrews 10:23).

GOD TEACHES THE ISRAELITES TO REFOCUS

Six weeks later, true to God's word,

people. A yearly celebration would be too easily forgotten. A once-a-month miracle would soon be overlooked. It's going to have to be a daily focusing—a constant reminder so powerfully significant that it will wake them up every day with grateful thoughts of God's faithful goodness:

> In your unfailing love you will lead
> > the people you have redeemed.
> In your strength you will guide
> > them (15:13).

What will the primary dynamics be for this refocusing strategy?

First of all, God wants His people to feel the constancy of His grace. In spite of the fact that they are

> a stubborn and rebellious generation
> whose hearts were not loyal to God,
> > whose spirits were not faithful to him (Psalm 78:8),

they have not been abandoned as they feared they would be. God wants them to know that He is a God of grace.

We're not just talking about ancient Israelites here. This is about us, too. It is in our weakness, not our strength, that God's power is made perfect, that His grace is demonstrated as fully sufficient (2 Corinthians 12:9). Paul makes the point again to the people in the churches in Ephesus and Rome and to you and me living in the twenty-first century:

As for you, you were dead in your transgressions and sins, in which you used to live when you followed the ways of this world and of the ruler of the kingdom of the air, the spirit who is now at work in those who are disobedient. All of us [notice there are no exceptions; Paul is speaking about *all of us*] also lived among them at one time, gratifying the cravings of our sinful nature and following its desires and thoughts. Like the rest, we were by nature objects of wrath. But because of his great love for us, God, who is rich in mercy, made us alive with Christ even when we were dead in transgressions—it is by grace you have been saved (Ephesians 2:1–5).

At just the right time, when we were still powerless, Christ died for the ungodly. Very rarely will anyone die for a righteous man, though for a good man someone might possibly dare to die. But God demonstrates his own love for us in this: While we were still sinners, Christ died for us (Romans 5:6–8).

Notice how *The Message* offers this passage:

Christ arrives right on time to make this happen. He didn't, and doesn't, wait for us to get ready. He presented himself for this sacrificial death when we were far too weak and rebellious to do anything to get ourselves ready. And even if we hadn't been so weak, we wouldn't have known what to do anyway. We can understand someone dying for a person worth dying for, and we can understand how someone good and noble could inspire us to selfless sacrifice. But God put his love on the line for us by offering his Son in sacrificial death while we were of no use whatever to him.

Why would God do such a thing? "Not because of anything we have done but because of his own purpose and grace. This grace was given us in Christ Jesus before the beginning of time" (2 Timothy 1:9). This is a crucial understanding. Notice when the grace is given. Not on our deathbed. Not once we settle securely into the truth. Not after our baptism. Not after we overcome our biggest temptation or after we obey all the commandments. "Before the beginning of time." Grace is never given as a reward for anything we do or don't do, including not complaining and not wishing we were back in Egypt and not grumbling about wandering in the wilderness. Our only qualification for grace is our great need—a need all of us humans share. God acts toward us in this gracious way because that's the kind of God He is and because He knows that fear of the judgment doesn't lead us to repentance; rather, we're led there by appreciation for His kindness (Romans 2:4).

Second, if our daily sustenance is from the gracious hand of God, then it follows that it is not "my power and the strength of my hands" that have produced "this wealth" (Deuteronomy 8:16, 17). I work, of course. But it is God who gives the power and the strength. He wants His children to learn that life is about so much more than just those things that we manage to produce. He meant His refocusing strategy to teach us that we don't "live on bread alone but on every word that comes from the mouth of the LORD" (Deuteronomy 8:3). Those things that perpetuate our earthly well-being—what we eat and drink, how we maintain our health, what we do each day to "make a living," how we clothe and shelter and provide for our families, and how we save for the future—all these are important topics for God's children every day of their lives on planet Earth. But there's a bigger picture we mustn't forget! "Don't fuss about what's on the table at mealtimes or whether the clothes in your closet are in fashion," Jesus instructs us. "There is far more to your life than the food you put in your stomach, more to your outer appearance than the clothes you hang on your body. Look at the birds, free and unfettered, not tied down to a job description, careless in the care of God. And you count far more to him than birds. . . . What I'm trying to do here," Jesus adds, "is to get you to relax, to not be so preoccupied with *getting,* so you can respond to God's *giving*" (Matthew 6:25–34, *The Message*).

Third, if it's true that the spirit of all prophetic utterance is to testify of Jesus (Revelation 19:10), if this Old Testament story is included when Jesus says, "The Scriptures . . . testify about me" (John 5:39), and if God's dealings with this mob of recently freed slaves might be part of what Jesus was talking about on the road to Emmaus when, "beginning with Moses and all the Prophets, he explained to them what was said in all the Scriptures concerning himself" (Luke 24:27), then this refocusing strategy must lead the children of Israel to the Lamb of God.

"Are you tired? Worn out?" Jesus asks. Are you sick of the severe circumstances and consequences of slavery? Are you weary with trudging through the wilderness every day of your life? Are you even "burned out on religion?

"Come to me," He invites. "Get away with me and you'll recover your life. I'll show you how to take a real rest. Walk with me and work with me—watch how I do it. Learn the unforced rhythms of grace. I won't lay anything heavy or ill-fitting on you. Keep company with me and you'll learn to live freely and lightly" (Matthew 11:28–30, *The Message*).

So here are the three dynamics in the strategy God is about to put into place to refocus His wandering children: it will reveal the God of grace, it will give rest from a preoccupation with getting so that there can be a response to God's giving, and it will shepherd the people to Jesus.

To accomplish these goals, God chooses to remind the people of an ancient observance, a gift that had been given many long centuries before their days in the wilderness, a gift they had ignored and forgotten in all those years of forced, seven-days-a-week labor in Egypt. He chooses to refocus them with the Sabbath. And He proposes to get to the Sabbath through something very dear to them—their stomachs!

"WHAT IS IT?"

The day before the strategy is introduced, Moses and Aaron instruct the people about what will begin the next day. They'll wake up to a sight no one in the world has ever seen before. When the layer of dew evaporates in the early warmth of the day, thin white flakes "like frost" will appear on the desert floor (Exodus 16:14, 31). The people soon begin calling this phenomenon *manna*—"What is it?" The psalmist refers to it as "the grain of heaven" and "the bread of angels" (Psalm 78:24, 25). Some say it tastes like "wafers made with honey" (Exodus 16:31) and others like "something made with olive oil" (Numbers 11:8).[1]

Every morning, you remember, the people were to gather enough manna to satisfy the hunger of their family for that day, and *only* for that day (Exodus 16:15–18). They could eat the manna just as they found it. They could grind it into flour, cook it in a pot, make it into cakes (Numbers 11:8), bake it or boil it (Exodus 16:23). But they were to gather only the amount they would use that day. As we have come to expect, some people in the camp tried to get around the instructions and do things their own way, with rotten results (16:20).

On the day before the Sabbath, the rules change. Now they are to gather enough for that day *plus* enough to eat the next day. No manna falls on the Sabbath, and the manna kept over from the previous day doesn't go bad. Once again, the Israelites experiment with gathering and preserving the manna their own way, until everyone finally comes to the realization that it just doesn't work to do it any other way than the way God outlined for them (16:23–30).

The purpose of the manna was not simply to feed the ravenous multitude every day. Every time the Israelites went out in the morning to gather manna, their realization that weekday mornings were fundamentally different from the morning of the Sabbath was to deepen. "The Sabbath is not for the sake of the weekdays," Abraham Joshua Heschel reminds us, "the weekdays are for the sake of Sabbath. It is not an interlude but the climax of living. . . . Six days a week we wrestle with the world, wringing profit from the earth; on the Sabbath we especially care for the seed of eternity planted in the soul. The world has our hands, but our soul belongs to Someone Else."[2]

Before the Ten Commandments were given from Sinai, the people learned to do all their work in six days and to rest in God's work on the seventh day, the Sabbath. On the Sabbath, there was to be no manna gathering. Manna was merely the means God used to call His children back to the observance of the Sabbath, to refocus them on His character and the mission He had in mind for them—to tell the world about the compassionate and gracious God who loves us and saves us (Psalm 103:1–14).

The manna experience is about the Sabbath. The Sabbath experience is about God's work in our lives and about our resting in His work. "There remains, then, a Sabbath-rest for the people of God; for anyone who enters God's rest also rests from his own work, just as God did from his" (Hebrews 4:9, 10). This awareness is so crucial to the formation of the identity of God's people, so important to the formation of a Christlike character, that God

instructed the Israelites to place a golden jar of manna in the ark of the covenant, along with the Ten Commandments, as a constant reminder of the refocusing strategy (Hebrews 9:4).

Manna is about Sabbath. Sabbath is about God's work in our lives. God's work brings us to Jesus. "I tell you the truth," Jesus said, "it is not Moses who has given you the bread from heaven, but it is my Father who gives you the true bread from heaven. For the bread of God is he who comes down from heaven and gives life to the world. . . . Just as the living Father sent me and I live because of the Father, so the one who feeds on me will live because of me. This is the bread that came down from heaven. Your forefathers ate manna and died, but he who feeds on this bread will live forever" (John 6:32, 33, 57, 58).

For the entire time the children of Israel wandered in the wilderness, during all those years in which God was attempting to re-create His image in the lives of His redeemed people, manna fell like rain (Psalm 78:24). "The Israelites ate manna forty years, until they came to a land that was settled; they ate manna until they reached the border of Canaan" (Exodus 16:35). "The manna stopped the day after they ate this food from the land; there was no longer any manna for the Israelites, but that year they ate of the produce of Canaan" (Joshua 5:12).

Israel's journey is our journey. For the entire time we wander here in this earthly wilderness, during all this time in which God is attempting to re-create the character of Jesus in our already redeemed lives, our day-by-day existence brings us to the Sabbath, and the Sabbath refocuses our identity as God's people, chosen by grace.

SABBATH IN THE END TIMES

As we move toward the final days of earth's history, end-time people will stay focused on resting in the work of God and on proclaiming the extraordinary message His last-day people give about God's grace. We need to be communicating a clear, compelling, personal answer to the question, "Who is this God that I should listen to Him?" Whenever we are tempted, like the ancient Hebrews, to turn that answer away from a description of what God has done and is doing in our lives and to focus instead on what we're doing or not doing, or on what human agencies or a combination of events are doing to try to thwart God's purpose on earth, it is the Sabbath that refocuses us. It brings us back to where we need to be.

It tests our commitment to biblical religion. As nothing else can, the Sabbath reinforces for us those three strategic dynamics that ground our spirituality:

- Sabbath invites us to celebrate God's grace.
- Sabbath reminds us to be less preoccupied with *getting* so we can respond to God's *giving*.
- Sabbath recenters our lives in Jesus.

With all that's riding on the Sabbath—the distinctiveness of God's character and our identity as His people, the formation of a Christlike character within us, our commitment to biblical religion, and our acceptance of the extraordinary mission God gives us—would anyone, anywhere be surprised to find that our enemy, the roaring lion who prowls around looking for someone to devour (1 Peter 5:8), would make a point of attacking the Sabbath? That's been happening since the war in heaven began thousands of years ago. It will continue as long as this planet remains.

What is most troubling to you about those attacks? Throughout the millennia of history, countless people have advocated different understandings of the Sabbath.

Contradictory opinions have led people in divergent directions of Sabbath observance, and even into believing that Sabbath sacredness has been done away with altogether. Angry debates have raged. Legislation has been enacted. Interrogations have taken place and frightened people into changing their minds. Force has been applied, until even the staunchest of believers has "confessed their error." The record is there for everyone to read alongside of and in contrast to the biblical ideal for this set-apart, sacred day. Over and over again, without the aid of Sabbath keepers and sometimes even without the knowledge that there are such people as Sabbath keepers, students discover the historical record and react with appropriate reason and resolve.

Unfortunately, however, as unquestionably troubling as all those external attacks have been, none of them is as disturbing as what *believers* have done to the Sabbath from the inside. Though it's difficult to believe, it's true: the greatest distractions from the central, encouraging, spiritual meaning of the Sabbath have been produced, not by skeptics or infidels, not by inquisitors or persecutors, not by zealous or ambitious religious systems, but by Sabbath proponents themselves!

In the Old Testament, God's chosen people began to emphasize regulations that restricted Sabbath behavior. Rules were created and enforced in an attempt to dictate exactly what specific conducts honored or dishonored the Sabbath and to control the Sabbath experience. Before long, it wasn't discovering the God of grace and responding to God's giving and recentering in the Lamb of God that was the absorbing focus of Sabbath instruction. Instead, it was *keeping the rules.*

In New Testament times, this behavioral approach to Sabbath observance was employed to distinguish between "us" and "them," between those who *truly* followed Jesus and those who only pretended to follow, or those who followed in error, or those who didn't follow at all. By the end of the first century, grace-oriented Christians were so sick of all the rules that they were deliberately disassociating themselves from the seventh-day Sabbath. The Sabbath had become so tied to a legalistic approach to religion that people could no longer see any redeeming value to it.

Embarrassingly, to this very day, we Sabbath keepers frequently continue to misdirect the Sabbath discussion. Many of us grew up with forceful injunctions about what we could do and what we must not do on God's holy day, and those rules became embedded in our thinking about the Sabbath. The stories people have told me about the Sabbath restrictions in their homes are startling. (I'm sure you can add your own stories.) The daily manna gathering that was supposed to help us anticipate and appreciate the Sabbath was somehow turned into a single day of frenetic preparation during which we had better get all our work done before the moment when the sun disappeared below the horizon or be at risk of suffering eternal consequences.

We have talked about the way other people relate to the Sabbath in words that have come across as callous aspersions, and we often have spoken those words without any Christlike regard for sensitive listeners who simply were trying to be true to their long-held beliefs. We have spent so much time advertising our convictions in terms of pagan influences and political intrigues, changing calendars and arrogant decrees, final battles and fearsome beasts, that, unfortunately, many people—believers and nonbelievers alike—are convinced that's what the Sabbath is all about.

This distressing emphasis has produced two results. In the first place, people find such a Sabbath emphasis to be unattractive and unrewarding, and they refuse to affiliate with any organization in which people

take pleasure in living like that. On an overnight flight from Auckland to Los Angeles recently, I sat next to a talkative young Christian man who was eager to have a friendly conversation. Upon finding out that I was a Seventh-day Adventist minister, however, he grew reflective and serious. "My mother used to work at an Adventist hospital," he commented. "She told me two things about Adventists: you don't drink coffee, and you're very legalistic about your Sabbath."

My heart sank. This young man and his mother had formed an impression of us that had nothing at all to do with our understanding of the gracious God we love and worship. All I could tell him was that we *have* struggled with legalism. It's certainly been true in my life. But I assured him that we are learning a better way, the biblical way, of trusting in grace alone for our salvation, and then, because of God's grace, responding to Him by living a life of worship. Surely there aren't many left who still think that we get to heaven because we don't drink coffee or because we go to church on Saturday.

The second result of a misdirected Sabbath emphasis involves people who once included the Sabbath as a joyous part of their experience but who have decided they no longer want to support Sabbath observance that is focused exclusively on what we can and can't do. Many of these people leave our community of faith—often with the most bitter of feelings—without realizing that what they are objecting to are *human* interpretations, not biblical ideals.

How sobering to think that Jesus might say to us as He said to the "Pharisees and teachers of the law" with all their ceremonies and rituals: "You have let go of the commands of God and are holding on to the traditions of men. . . . You nullify the word of God by your tradition that you have handed down" (Mark 7:5–13). Paul learned that being "extremely zealous for the traditions" wasn't what God wanted for him. Rather, He wanted him to reveal Jesus to those who approach God from a different direction (Galatians 1:13–16).

TESTED BY THE SABBATH

End-time people will be tested by the Sabbath. At the close of earth's history, the message will be proclaimed that righteousness and justification and salvation are by grace alone, through faith alone, in Jesus Christ alone.[3] "And if by grace, then it is no longer by works; if it were, grace would no longer be grace" (Romans 11:6). The Sabbath is a banner that announces our worship of the God of grace and testifies to our assurance that our salvation is because of *Christ's righteousness,* not ours. The final remnant—"a remnant chosen by grace"—will, by remembering the Sabbath, joyfully testify to *God's* loyalty and faithfulness to His earth-bound people. The Sabbath will be set before the world "in its true light"[4] and will disclose to all people that it is God who makes us holy—that we never can obtain holiness by ourselves (Ezekiel 20:12).

Just as the daily gift of the manna pointed people to the Sabbath, so the Sabbath, when we have given it its rightful place in our lives, is a recurring gift to point people to the God of grace. It is the profound mission of end-time people to proclaim God's glory and righteousness with a loud voice to every nation, tribe, language, and people (Revelation 14:6). In the process, we enable the fourth commandment to testify about Jesus.

The message of end-time people is not about what we do or don't do to try to be obedient. It's not about us! We love the Sabbath because we love Jesus in the Sabbath. We keep the commandments of God *and* we hold to the testimony of Jesus (14:12; 19:10). The Bible clearly instructs us: "To the law and to the testimony!" (Isaiah 8:20). If we do not elevate Jesus in the Sabbath, we fail the test of commitment to biblical religion. But when we allow the Sabbath to speak of God's enduring grace, people are drawn to Jesus. "Our confession of His faithfulness is Heaven's chosen agency for revealing Christ to the world. We are to acknowledge His grace as made known through the holy men of old; but that which will be most effectual is the testimony of our own experience."[5]

The three dynamics in the strategy God has put into place to keep His wandering children fully focused on Him remain the same in the end times. All the daily manna-gathering activities of our lives bring us to the Sabbath. The Sabbath reveals to us a God of grace. It gives us rest from a preoccupation with getting so that we can respond to God's giving. It keeps us centered in Jesus, the Lamb of God who takes away the sin of the world.

This is what the Lord Almighty says: "I will cleanse them from all the sin they have committed against me and will forgive all their sins of rebellion against me. . . . I will fulfill the gracious promise I made to the house of Israel and to the house of Judah" (Jeremiah 33:8, 14). In those final days on earth, we will discern "the sounds of joy and gladness, the voices of bride and bridegroom, and the voices of those who bring thank offerings to the house of the LORD, saying,

'Give thanks to the LORD Almighty,
　　for the LORD is good;
　　his love endures forever.' . . .
'In those days and at that time
　　I will make a righteous Branch
　　　　sprout from David's line;
　　he will do what is just and
　　　　right in the land.
In those days Judah will be saved
　　and Jerusalem will live in
　　　　safety.
This is the name by which it will
　　be called:
The LORD Our Righteous-
　　ness' " (33:11, 15, 16).

"*His* dominion is an everlasting dominion that will not pass away, and *his* kingdom is one that will never be destroyed" (Daniel 7:14).

That everlasting, indestructible kingdom is the kingdom of God's never-failing, always-enduring grace. The Sabbath is a banner announcing our part in that kingdom. It is a loud voice proclaiming our allegiance to the One who sits upon the throne of grace. As we begin to experience the Sabbath as a delight, we realize that our deepest joy is found in the unconditional love of our heavenly Parent. When we quit insisting on following our own traditions for this precious day, we begin to truly honor Him who gives us the Sabbath gift. With joy we hear God's voice saying,

> I will cause you to ride on the
> heights of the land
> and to feast on the inheritance of
> your father Jacob,

and we begin to possess the land that has been given to us by grace (Isaiah 58:14).

We know the promise is true, not because we have remembered the Sabbath or correctly kept it or courageously stood up for it, but because it is God who has promised it, and by His grace He makes it so.

---

1. In rabbinical teaching, the fact that some Israelites thought the manna tasted like honey and others were sure it was something made with olive oil was an indication that the taste of the manna conformed to each Israelite's favorite flavor. The rabbis used this manna story to show that when God created Paradise, He kept in mind the desires of each person's heart.

2. Abraham Joshua Heschel, *The Sabbath* (New York: Farrar, Straus and Giroux, 1951), 13, 14.

3. "Several have written to me, inquiring if the message of justification by faith is the third angel's message, and I have answered, 'It is the third angel's message in verity.'" Ellen G. White, *Evangelism,* 190.

4. White, *The Great Controversy* (Mountain View, Calif.: Pacific Press®, 1950), 605.

5. White, *The Ministry of Healing* (Mountain View, Calif.: Pacific Press®, 1909), 100.

Vision Number Seven
Matthew 25:1–13

"At that time the kingdom of heaven will be like ten virgins who took their lamps and went out to meet the bridegroom. Five of them were foolish and five were wise. The foolish ones took their lamps but did not take any oil with them. The wise, however, took oil in jars along with their lamps. The bridegroom was a long time in coming, and they all became drowsy and fell asleep.

"At midnight the cry rang out: 'Here's the bridegroom! Come out to meet him!'

"Then all the virgins woke up and trimmed their lamps. The foolish ones said to the wise, 'Give us some of your oil; our lamps are going out.'

" 'No,' they replied, 'there may not be enough for both us and you. Instead, go to those who sell oil and buy some for yourselves.'

"But while they were on their way to buy the oil, the bridegroom arrived. The virgins who were ready went in with him to the wedding banquet. And the door was shut.

"Later the others also came. 'Sir! Sir!' they said. 'Open the door for us!'

"But he replied, 'I tell you the truth, I don't know you.'

"Therefore keep watch, because you do not know the day or the hour."

THEY DON'T SEEM TO HAVE NOTICED

How would we react if Jesus appeared in our town today? Would we recognize Him? Or are we too distracted by all the demands of the busy lives we lead? Would we welcome Him? Or would we wish He would go away so we could get on with more important matters?

It's 1888.

In Minneapolis, Minnesota, delegates to the Adventist ministerial institute and General Conference session meet to discuss the impact on their beliefs of a recently agitated public dispute about the righteousness of Christ. In America's capital city, where Benjamin Harrison has just been elected as the nation's twenty-third president, the Washington Monument officially opens. In London, the bodies of the first victims of the serial killer known as Jack the Ripper are discovered. In France, during a bout with mental illness, Vincent van Gogh cuts off a portion of his left ear.

And in Belgium, another young artist puts the finishing touches on a monumental, controversial painting that keeps us marveling at his meaning and purpose to this very day.[1]

James Ensor was considered avant-garde by the late-nineteenth-century art community.

Still in the process of learning to appreciate the supple, radiant impressions of Monet, Renoir, and Degas, few people were ready for a further development in artistic vogue. Van Gogh, Gauguin, Cézanne, and Seurat were already experimenting in radical directions and hearing heckles. But Ensor had been captured by a vision. Dismissing the objections of the critics, he hurled himself into an expressive project that would directly confront the religious indifference of the people of his country.

In the little attic studio in his family home in Ostend, there were no walls large enough to hold the canvas the twenty-eight-year-old artist envisioned. Ensor rearranged the room, pushing furniture to the side, and then he spread a sprawling eight-by-fourteen-foot

James Ensor, *Christ's Entry Into Brussels in 1889*
To view this painting in color, go to www.pacificpress.com/chosenbygrace.

canvas on the floor. Sitting on and crawling over the canvas, Ensor attacked his carefully organized composition. Using a crayon, he positioned hundreds of characters marching in an enormous parade that proceeded from a distant point in the upper right portion of the scene and wound through the boulevards of Brussels until the marchers spilled out over the entire foreground, ready to walk over any viewer standing in their way. Then, with palette knives and spatulas and both ends of his paintbrushes, Ensor aggressively applied audacious patches of vigorous color. "White! More white!" the artist called. "The pure color. The one that brings things to the fore without betraying it. Vivid red. Green green. Raw yellow."

Building on an artistic tradition known as "the joyous entry," Ensor began painting a Mardi Gras scene: a riot of carnival revelers, most wearing silly or grotesque masks. The resultant mob has been described as "a crude, ugly, chaotic, dehumanized sea of masks, frauds, clowns, and caricatures." Following a swaggering, rotund drum major wearing a bishop's miter, the crowd celebrates an unrestrained festival. A uniformed, slow-witted marching band blares away in an inaudible racket. Placards wave in the air. Spectators cheer. Bedlam reigns.

But what's that just to the left of center? Is it another mask? No, it's a brown animal with long ears—a donkey tramping among the people, some of whom are arrogantly raising their noses in complete disdain, while others apparently are bowing to the figure riding on the donkey. The bearded rider is robed in red and gray. His eyes are calm, not frantic like the surrounding rabble. His right arm is stretched out in a gesture that seems to offer serenity and peace. A yellow halo surrounds his head.

Oh! It's Jesus!

And now the message of the painting begins to come into focus. Ensor, you remember, completes this project in 1888. But he titles his painting *Christ's Entry into Brussels in 1889*.

In a prophetic statement, speaking with forceful authority as well as with prescience, Ensor portrays what he believes are the religious and political realities of his time and his people. If Jesus Himself appeared in their city, Ensor states, the people of Brussels, distracted and hiding behind disguises, would be "too involved in their own strutting and revelry to acknowledge the presence of the Christian Savior." Perhaps they'd hold up a sign on which they had hastily scribbled, "Long live Jesus, King of Brussels," but the arrival of the King of kings wouldn't really capture their attention. Author Stephen Farthing observes, "They don't seem to have noticed."

Christ's Entry into Brussels in 1889 was created at the height of a European theological debate that swirled around the nature of Jesus. Positivist philosophers were declaring that Jesus was simply a historical figure full of admirable wisdom and moral greatness—a spiritual genius and a charismatic social leader to be sure, but definitely not divine.

French philosopher Émile Littré, who appears prominently and unmistakably in an Ensor drawing from 1885, an early version of this same setting, considered the church to be an oppressive institution that led people astray with its "mythology" of the preexistence of Christ. Littré translated David Strauss's *Life of Jesus,* which argues not only that Jesus wasn't divine but also that He wasn't even Jewish! In fact, wrote Strauss, He was actually an Aryan. Thus, Strauss's book laid the groundwork for future anti-Semitic theories. Albert Schweitzer said these conclusions about the nature of Christ were the most important contributions of nineteenth-century German theology. The Getty Center's notes on *Christ's Entry into Brussels in 1889* identifies the central drum major as Littré, "leading on the eager, mindless crowd"—an assertive bishop in a new, Christless religion.

Ensor forces the viewer of his monumental painting to search for Jesus. Almost concealed by the colorful swarm of merrymakers, almost obscured by the dissonant compositional vanishing points, almost overlooked, Jesus remains at the heart of what we learn from Ensor's painting.[1]

Is Jesus central to our spirituality? Is He the principal focus of our theology? Do we hide behind masks that indicate other priorities? Do we get distracted, sometimes by other "good" things? Sometimes even by "getting ready" for His appearing?

---

1. The Ensor painting resides at the Getty Museum in Los Angeles, California. For a thorough description of the painting and its background, see James Ensor, *Christ's Entry Into Brussels in 1889* (Los Angeles: Getty Publications, 2002). Unless otherwise noted, quotations referring to Ensor and this painting are from this publication.

READY FOR THE BRIDEGROOM

Why does the Bridegroom delay His coming? What causes the darkness of the end times? How do we know if we are ready for the Bridegroom's return? What does it mean to wake up? To be on guard? To keep watch?

When it came to the topic of the Second Coming, the disciples were full of questions. But in their conversations with Jesus, one element of His return was perfectly clear to them. It made a lasting impression: the Second Coming is going to happen unexpectedly, like a robbery in the middle of the night.

"If the owner of the house had known at what time of night the thief was coming, he would have kept watch." Matthew quotes the words with a warning (Matthew 24:42–44). Mark and Luke make the point abundantly clear: "You do not know when that time will come" (Mark 13:32–37; Luke 12:40). John incorporates the image into his message to the churches of Revelation: "I will come like a thief" (Revelation 3:3). Peter says it again: "The day of the Lord will come like a thief" (2 Peter 3:9–18). Paul "gets the memo" from the disciples, restates the picture, and reminds his readers they already know what he's talking about (1 Thessalonians 5:1–11).

Jesus is coming back when we least expect it. Like a thief in the middle of the night.

"You do not know on what day your Lord will come," Jesus tells us (Matthew 24:36–44). He says no one knows about that day or hour. He doesn't know. The angels in heaven don't know. It will happen suddenly. It will be a surprise. Like a thief.

BETWEEN NOW AND THEN

The disciples catch one more thing from their conversations: between now and then, there's going to be what feels like a delay. "The bridegroom was a long time in coming" (Matthew 25:5).

No matter what the reason for the delay, no matter how exciting the event at the end of the waiting period is, the delay still feels . . . well, unfortunate; even perhaps a little bit annoying. It's like the feeling you get when you have to stand in a long line at the bank or the post office or you have to wait who knows how long to get into your favorite restaurant—only much worse. And as so often happens during a delay, especially a delay at night, we get drowsy. We go to sleep. Foolish people get drowsy and go to sleep. Wise people get drowsy and go to sleep (Matthew 25:5). It's natural. There's certainly nothing wrong with becoming drowsy or going to sleep.

While I was in college, a friend invited me to drive to San Francisco with him on a Sunday morning, go to Grace Cathedral in the middle of the city, and hear a sermon by the great Protestant theologian Paul Tillich. I worked the graveyard shift in a hospital, so I realized I would be tired when I got off work. But I really did want to hear Tillich.

When I finished my shift at the hospital, I changed my clothes and, without any sleep, got in my friend's car and headed to the city. We talked all the way there about the exciting opportunity and about how Tillich's theology had inspired us. We arrived early to be sure to get a good seat. We sat through an early church service. We got more excited as Tillich's service began. We stood and sang the hymns. We read along with the Scripture readings. At last, Tillich ascended the pulpit. It was a little after eleven in the morning. I took out the paper I had brought along so I could take notes. Tillich began to preach. And I went to sleep!

Imagine for a moment that instead of telling us the parable of the wise and foolish virgins who all get drowsy and go to sleep while they're waiting for the bridegroom to appear, Jesus had likened the kingdom of heaven to a college student who was waiting to hear a famous theologian. (Since Jesus likened the kingdom to so many other things—a mustard seed, a treasure hidden in a field, a merchant looking for fine pearls, a net that was let down into a lake, a king who wanted to settle accounts with his servants—likening the kingdom to a college student isn't at all far-fetched, is it?) If Jesus had told us that while the college student was waiting, he got drowsy and went to sleep, that would be the easy part of the parable to understand, don't you agree? But what about the next part? What do you think Jesus would advise the college student to do?

In other places in the Bible where we hear conversations about the thief in the middle of the night, we hear counsel such as this: "Wake up" (Revelation 3:2; 16:15). "Be on your guard!" (2 Peter 3:17). "Keep watch" (Matthew 24:42; 25:13). "Be ready" (Luke 12:40).

Obviously, if the college student wanted

"The people walking in darkness
    have seen a great light;
on those living in the land of the
    shadow of death
    a light has dawned" (Isaiah 9:2).

"The light shines in the darkness, but the darkness has not understood it" (John 1:5).

"I have come into the world as a light, so that no one who believes in me should stay in darkness" (John 12:46).

"I am sending you to them to open their eyes and turn them from darkness to light, and from the power of Satan to God, so that they may receive forgiveness of sins and a place among those who are sanctified by faith in me" (Acts 26:17, 18).

"God, who said, 'Let light shine out of darkness,' made his light shine in our hearts to give us the light of the knowledge of the glory of God in the face of Christ" (2 Corinthians 4:6).

to hear the sermon, he should have been awake and alert! Perhaps he should have taken off work the previous night and gotten a good night's sleep. Or at least he should have taken a nap on the trip to San Francisco instead of talking all the way.

But if the parable is about the delay between Christ's promise to return and the Second Coming and we're trying to figure out what we should be doing to be ready for that return, isn't it also obvious that Jesus isn't talking about actual, "close your eyes and breathe deeply" sleep? He's not telling us that the people at the end of time who are ready for Jesus to return are a bunch of insomniacs. The formula for being ready doesn't include a lot of extra caffeine. "Wake up" doesn't mean, "Don't go to sleep."

WAKE UP!

In Jesus' parable of the ten virgins (Matthew 25:1–13), the bridegroom doesn't arrive until midnight, when the girls are all asleep and the night is full of darkness. If we understand what darkness means in the Bible, we'll start to grasp what it really means to wake up.

Let's begin with Paul. He instructs us that it is people who sleep in the darkness and get drunk in the darkness who also get *surprised* in the darkness. Paul also insists that followers of Jesus belong to the day not to the night or to the darkness. Followers of Jesus are children of the light and the day. We aren't in darkness, Paul reasons, so the Second Coming shouldn't surprise us like a thief (1 Thessalonians 5:1–11).

Light and darkness constitute an ancient biblical theme. Look at the Creation story, take it for its *spiritual* significance, and we see God's original initiative is separating light from darkness. That's His very first act for the people of this planet (Genesis 1:4). From that moment on, God has been calling humans "out of darkness into his wonderful light" (1 Peter 2:9). He has qualified us "to share in the inheritance of the saints in the kingdom of light. For he has rescued us from the dominion of darkness and brought us into the kingdom of the Son he loves" (Colossians 1:12, 13). Jesus is the Light of the world. Whoever follows Jesus "will never walk in darkness" (John 8:12). "If you have received the grace of God, the light is in you. Remove the obstructions, and the Lord's glory will be revealed. The light will shine forth, to penetrate and dispel the darkness."[1]

The kingdom of light is the kingdom of Jesus. The kingdom of darkness is the realm of our enemy. Jesus explained to Paul that He was sending him to turn people from darkness to light, to help them "see the difference between Satan and God, and choose God." The appointed content for this mission was to present God's "offer of sins forgiven" (Acts 26:18, *The Message*). It's the same mission God has given us all: "Carry the light-giving Message into the night" (Philippians 2:15, 16, *The Message*).

To "wake up" means, first of all, to begin to grasp the fundamental differences between spiritual darkness and spiritual light, between Satan and God, between the kingdom of darkness and the kingdom of light. To "wake up" is to make the choice between the enemy's deceptive assertions about God and His government (the position of those who are asleep in the darkness) and Christ's assuring portrayal of the forgiving character of His gracious Father (accepted by those who are awake and in the light).

And there's something more— something absolutely fascinating—about this "wake up and come into the light" analogy in the Bible. Just before the great Armageddon battle, according to Revelation 16, Jesus announces again, "Behold, I come like a thief! Blessed is he who stays awake." But this time Jesus adds that he is blessed who stays awake and *"keeps his clothes with him"* (16:15). Not only does this wake-up command mean to accept God's forgiveness, it also has something to do with being properly clothed.

Paul was particularly fond of this picture. "Clothe yourselves with the Lord Jesus Christ," he counsels us (Romans 13:14). When we are baptized into Christ, he says, we are clothed with Christ (Galatians 3:27). Paul also speaks of being "clothed with our heavenly dwelling," our "eternal house in heaven," and he says we can have full assurance that we are properly clothed because God "has given us the Spirit as a deposit, guaranteeing

what is to come." Therefore, Paul concludes, because we wear the clothes God has given us instead of wearing our own clothes, "we are always confident" (2 Corinthians 5:1–7).

Christ's parable of the wedding garment tells the same story (Matthew 22:1–13). The guest who tries to sneak into the banquet in his own clothes is caught and thrown out "into the darkness" ("outer darkness," the King James Version puts it). Jesus makes it clear that no one will be permitted to enter the banquet unless they are wearing the robe Christ gives to them. In her commentary about this parable, Ellen White makes the unforgettable statement, "This robe, woven in the loom of heaven, has in it not one thread of human devising."[2]

There's also the significant story in the First Testament's book of Zechariah about how the assurance of salvation is the robe given us. The high priest of the people, a man named Joshua, you remember, is standing before God in judgment, with Satan assuming the role of prosecuting attorney and pointing out Joshua's many sins. But when the Judge speaks, it is Satan who is rebuked, not Joshua, whom God refers to as "a burning stick snatched from the fire" (Zechariah 3:2).

Then this breathtaking passage:

> "Daily expect the Day of God, *eager for its arrival.* The galaxies will burn up and the elements melt down that day—but we'll hardly notice. We'll be looking the other way, *ready for* the promised new heavens and the promised new earth, all landscaped with righteousness.
>
> "So, my dear friends, since this is what you have to *look forward to . . .*" (2 Peter 3:12–14, *The Message*).
>
> "While you wait and *earnestly long for* (expect and hasten) the coming of the day of God" (2 Peter 3:12, AMP).
>
> "You should *look forward to* the day when God judges everyone" (2 Peter 3:12, CEV).

Now Joshua was dressed in filthy clothes as he stood before the angel. The angel said to those who were standing before him,

"Rejoice in the LORD and be glad,
  you righteous;
sing, all you who are upright
  in heart!" (Psalm 32:11).

"May all who seek you
  rejoice and be glad in you;
may those who love your salvation
  always say,
  'The Lord be exalted!' " (Psalm 40:16).

"May the righteous be glad
  and rejoice before God;
may they be happy and joyful"
  (Psalm 68:3).

"The ransomed of the LORD
  will return.
They will enter Zion with singing;
  everlasting joy will crown their
  heads.
Gladness and joy will overtake them,
  and sorrow and sighing will flee
  away" (Isaiah 35:10).

"Sing, O Daughter of Zion;
  shout aloud, O Israel!
Be glad and rejoice with all your heart,
  O Daughter of Jerusalem!
The LORD has taken away your
  punishment,
he has turned back your enemy"
  (Zephaniah 3:14, 15).

"Take off his filthy clothes."

Then he said to Joshua, "See, I have taken away your sin, and I will put rich garments on you" (3:3, 4).

Putting on the rich garments means trusting God to take away our sin rather than trying to do anything to contribute to what Christ already has done. Ellen White observes, "Zechariah's vision of Joshua and the Angel applies with peculiar force to the experience of God's people in the closing scenes of the great day of atonement."[3] Regarding the point of that vision, she says, "Israel was clothed with 'change of raiment'—the righteousness of Christ imputed to them. . . . He who was the hope of Israel then, their defense, their justification and redemption, is the hope of the church today. . . . All who have put on the robe of Christ's righteousness will stand before Him as chosen and faithful and true. Satan has no power to pluck them out of the hand of the Saviour."[4]

The Bible's teaching is that to wake up is to become aware of the differences between the kingdom of darkness and the kingdom of light. Then, when God's pursuing grace has captured us and we begin to see "the light of the knowledge of the glory of God in the face of Christ"

(2 Corinthians 4:6), we accept the grace of our forgiving God. We allow God to clothe us in Jesus. We hold on to His rich garment of righteousness. We become confident that our sin has been taken away. We are at peace knowing that the Holy Spirit guarantees our eternal home.

To be awake in the biblical sense is to stand in the light of the knowledge that we are saved by grace alone, and because of that awareness, to have the joyful assurance of salvation.

BE ON GUARD!

The "thief in the night" references also are not meant to indicate that the Second Coming will take place at night, or quietly, or that we will be unaware of His return as it is happening. Listen to how Jesus describes that day: "As lightning that comes from the east is visible even in the west, so will be the coming of the Son of Man" (Matthew 24:27). He says that all the nations of the earth "will see the Son of Man coming on the clouds of the sky, with power and great glory. And he will send his angels with a loud trumpet call, and they will gather his elect from the four winds, from one end of the heavens to the other" (24:30, 31).

No one's going to be sleeping through that!

Paul tells us, "The Lord himself will come down from heaven, with a loud command, with the voice of the archangel and with the trumpet call of God" (1 Thessalonians 4:16). Peter adds to the picture:

> The day of the Lord will come like a thief. The heavens will disappear with a roar; the elements will be destroyed by fire, and the earth and everything in it will be laid bare. . . .
>
> Therefore, dear friends, since you already know this, be on your guard (2 Peter 3:10, 17).

Peter's chapter-long passage about the thief in the night and about being on guard clearly is placed in an end-time setting. Peter explains that this will happen "in the last days" (3:3). Scoffers will laugh about the delay in the Second Coming (3:4). The day of judgment will take place (3:7). "The day of the Lord will come like a thief" (3:10). And then, in the middle of five short verses full of destruction, fire, and the elements melting in the heat (3:10–14), three separate times Peter uses the unexpected phrase "looking forward to"

(3:12–14), as if this climactic end-time event is really something we should enthusiastically and joyfully be longing for!

Paul employs the same perspective over and over again: "As you *eagerly wait* for our Lord Jesus Christ to be revealed" (1 Corinthians 1:7). "We *wait eagerly* for our adoption as [children], the redemption of our bodies. For in this hope we are saved" (Romans 8:23, 24). "Our citizenship is in heaven. And we *eagerly await* a Savior from there, the Lord Jesus Christ" (Philippians 3:20).

We've talked about this before, in chapter 1, but I don't think it can be overstated. For those who trust in the salvation that is given by the grace of God alone, for those who have been clothed in the robe of Christ's righteousness and are living in the light of God's forgiveness, the thoughts of Peter and Paul are exactly right—the expectation of the Second Coming brings gladness and rejoicing and song (Psalm 32:11), not fear or dread.

If our being on guard leads us into gladness and rejoicing, if it makes us eagerly anticipate the Second Coming, then *to be on guard* must mean to hold on to our trust that God has all the power He needs to fulfill His promises to us (Romans 4:20, 21). It means that we fully put our faith in the fact of Jesus' return,

in the gift of eternal life, and in the knowledge that God gives that gift to us *by grace alone.*

"Do not let your hearts be troubled," Jesus pleads with us. "Trust in God; trust also in me. In my Father's house are many rooms; if it were not so, I would have told you. I am going there to prepare a place for you. And if I go and prepare a place for you, I will come back and take you to be with me that you also may be where I am" (John 14:1–3).

> In him we have redemption through his blood, the forgiveness of sins, in accordance with the riches of God's grace. . . .
>
> . . . Having believed, you were marked in him with a seal, the promised Holy Spirit, who is a deposit guaranteeing our inheritance until the redemption of those who are God's possession (Ephesians 1:7, 13, 14).

To be on guard means—note this carefully now—to not "fall from *your secure position,*" your assurance about your salvation, but, instead, to "grow in the grace and knowledge of our Lord and Savior Jesus Christ" (2 Peter 3:17, 18).

KEEP WATCH!

What does it mean for us to keep watch? An ancient story helps us understand.

In the middle of the sixth century B.C., Croesus (pronounced *CREE-sus*), the king of Lydia who ruled from its capital city of Sardis, was one of the wealthiest monarchs in the world. During the time of Croesus, the neighboring kingdoms were in turmoil. The Assyrians had been defeated. The neo-Babylonian empire was in decline. The Median people were retreating. The Persians were just beginning to flex their muscles. Croesus saw an opportunity for expansion.

At the time, the Halys River was the border between Lydia and Media. Croesus planned to invade the Median portion of the Persian Empire, of which Cyrus was king, by crossing the Halys River at the city of Pteria in northern Cappadocia (in modern Turkey). The battle that followed, usually dated to about 546 B.C., ended with massive casualties on both sides, but it was inconclusive. Croesus retreated to Sardis, followed swiftly by Cyrus.

The story is told that, after a two-week siege of Sardis, a soldier in the Persian army by the name of Hyeroeades (*higher-o-E-a-deez*), made a strategic discovery. He noticed one afternoon that way up on the wall that protected Sardis, fifteen hundred feet above the plain where the Persian army was camped, a sentry carelessly dropped his helmet, which tumbled all the way down the mountain and landed just beyond the Persian camp. Sometime later, the sentry suddenly appeared on the plain, quickly retrieved his helmet, and then disappeared back up the mountain.

Hyeroeades secretly followed the sentry and discovered a hidden pathway that led all the way to the gate of the city. That night, in the cover of darkness, the Persians ascended the pathway and found the gates to the city open and unguarded, with no one keeping watch, no one looking out for the enemy. The Persians crept into Sardis, captured it, and put an end to the Lydian empire.

Utilizing this very history, John the revelator appeals to the young Christian church at Sardis at the end of the first century A.D., asking them to "be watchful" (Revelation 3:2, KJV). And if the people in the church don't watch, John warns, Jesus "will come like a thief," and they will not be ready (3:3).

The ancient people of the city of Sardis relied on their own strength and what they considered to be the secure unassailability of their position to protect them against the Persians. They thought they could go home and go to bed and not even watch for the enemy.

Likewise, the first-century Christian people of the church of Sardis had become self-reliant. They thought they were alive, but, in fact, they already were dead. They were counting on their reputation and their good works to guard them against their spiritual enemy, to provide security, and to assure deliverance in the day of judgment (3:1, 2).

For our part, we too often follow the bad example of those first-century Christians at Sardis. We too easily put our trust for deliverance in things other than Jesus, things that we produce ourselves: our good reputation (notice the nice compliments Dan Buettner gives us in his 2008 book, *The Blue Zones*); our good deeds (mission trips, hospitals, schools, community service); our growing activism (in such things as religious freedom, HIV/AIDS education and treatment, and ecology); our commitment to evangelism (and the number of people joining our church every year); and the strong, rational foundation of our doctrines. All those things are good things, splendid things, fitting things for the followers of Jesus. But when we turn any of them or all of them into even a hint of a contribution that we make to our salvation, they become like the good works of

the church at Sardis: dead instead of alive, not in any way meriting salvation. "I have not found your deeds complete in the sight of my God" (3:2).

There were, however, a few in Sardis who instead were following Jesus. In describing them, John says, They "have not defiled their garments" (3:4, KJV), and then the prophet repeats Christ's promise: "He who overcomes will, like them, be dressed in white. I will never blot out his name from the book of life, but will acknowledge his name before my Father" (3:5).

Keep watch.

Don't defile your garments.

Overcome.

Know that your name is written in the book of life, the book "belonging to the Lamb that was slain from the creation of the world" (13:8).

Each of these descriptions means the same thing. Relying on Jesus for our deliverance. Being dressed in the robe of His righteousness alone. Overcoming the temptation to try to contribute to our salvation. Being assured that our names are written in the Lamb's book of life because we are engraved on the palms of His hands (Isaiah 49:16).

When my name comes up in the final judgment, the angel will turn in the book to the page of accumulated sins, and though they have been many, the angel will say, "It's blank except for the notation 'See Jesus.' " And when the page is turned to the one where good works are recorded, the angel will say the same thing: "It's blank except for the notation 'See Jesus.' "

The Bible has invited us to be confident of our eternal standing, to know that our salvation is sure, because "he who promised is faithful" (Hebrews 10:19–23).

That's *how* we keep watch.

And we don't know when that day or hour will take place (Matthew 24:42–44; 25:13; Mark 13:35–37). That's *why* we keep watch.

BE READY!

Sometimes, unfortunately, it seems we quit being awake, quit being on guard, and quit keeping watch. We lose the focus on what is central to our spirituality. Like the people of Brussels in James Ensor's painting, we hide behind masks that reveal that we have other priorities. We get distracted, even by the good things we do.

And often the biggest distraction seems to be what we think we must yet accomplish in "getting ready" for the Second Coming. I've heard that phrase since I was a child, and I always interpreted it in terms of things I needed to do before Jesus returns. I had to keep the Sabbath more carefully. I had to be a more cheerful giver. I had to be sweeter to the most difficult people I knew. I had to study my Bible more regularly and pray more consistently. I had to overcome my temptations more thoroughly. Getting ready was what I had to do to make God love me enough that He would wink at my sin and reward me with eternal life anyway.

Of course, I want to keep the Sabbath and be more cheerful and sweeter and study my Bible and pray more consistently and overcome the temptations that come my way. But that's not what the Bible means by "being ready" (see Luke 12:40).

Being ready means waking up. Waking up means accepting the grace of Jesus.

Being ready means being on guard. Being on guard means being clothed in the righteousness of Christ and holding on to the assurance of our salvation, which is given by grace alone.

Being ready means keeping watch. Keeping watch means being assured that by grace our names are written in the Lamb's book of life.

Being ready means resting securely in God's grace alone, now, and in the end times.

1. Ellen G. White, *Christ's Object Lessons* (Washington, D.C.: Review and Herald®, 1941), 420.

2. Ibid., 311. "By the wedding garment in the parable is represented the pure, spotless character which Christ's true followers will possess. . . . It is the righteousness of Christ, His own unblemished character, that through faith is imparted to all who receive Him as their personal Savior" (Ibid., 310).

3. White, *Prophets and Kings,* 587.

4. Ibid., 584, 585, 587. Note also: "[Joshua's] own sins and those of his people were pardoned. Israel was clothed with 'change of raiment'—the righteousness of Christ imputed to them" (page 584). "He who was the hope of Israel then, their defense, their justification and redemption, is the hope of the church today" (page 585). "Through the plan of salvation, Jesus is breaking Satan's hold upon the human family, and rescuing souls from his power. . . . With fiendish power and cunning [Satan] works to wrest from Him the children of men who have accepted salvation. . . .

"Satan knows that those who ask God for pardon and grace will obtain it; therefore he presents their sins before them to discourage them" (page 586).

"It is the privilege of every soul to be a living channel through which God can communicate to the world the treasures of His grace, the unsearchable riches of Christ. There is nothing that Christ desires so much as agents who will represent to the world His Spirit and character. There is nothing that the world needs so much as the manifestation through humanity of the Saviour's love. All heaven is waiting for channels through which can be poured the holy oil to be a joy and blessing to human hearts" (419).

"In their own life and character [followers of Christ] are to reveal what the grace of God has done for them" (416).

"If you have received the grace of God, the light is in you. Remove the obstructions, and the Lord's glory will be revealed. The light will shine forth to penetrate and dispel the darkness. You cannot help shining within the range of your influence" (420).

—Ellen White, *Christ's Object Lessons*

THE CORRIDOR OF GRACE

O n the lower level of the La Sierra University church, directly beneath the sanctuary, is a long, empty corridor that leads to several children's Sabbath School divisions. From the lobby of the church on the south side of the building, twenty-five narrow steps descend down, around to the right, and down again to the lower level. During each week, between Sabbath services, that corridor is one of the quietest, loneliest places on the church campus.

The corridor leads to the back of the building on the north side. It is poorly lit and nondescript; just a long hallway with no distinguishing features, no windows, and no doors until you get to the very end. There are no decorations on the walls, just numerous layers of that familiar, dingy, institutional off-white paint. Walking the length of the corridor is not something you'd want to do in the dark, but if you did, a little red fire extinguisher finally would stop you. It hangs on the wall at the end of the hallway under a sign that says, "In case of fire . . ."

Over the many years that the church has stood there on Sierra Vista Avenue in Riverside, California, tens of thousands of children have walked down that long hallway to go to Sabbath School. Inside the Sabbath School rooms, gifted children's ministry volunteers, using the denomination's *Gracelink* curriculum, lead the children in a deepening friendship with Jesus. But outside of the rooms, the hallway contributes nothing. It just takes you from here to there.

One day a couple of years ago, in search of an illustration for an upcoming sermon, I paused at that quiet, lonely spot at the bottom of the steps and looked down the length of the hallway. I began thinking about how similar the corridor is to the spiritual journeys we each take, from where we are at this moment in our lives to where we ultimately want to be—in heaven with Jesus for eternity. Often our journey is dark. Sometimes it's quiet and lonely. From time to time, there are children running all over the place. Every now and then, we seem to be sure of our destination. At other times, we're tempted to think we're not really going anywhere. And no matter what time it is, we'd rather not walk alone in the darkness.

I wondered whether we're really destined to wander through a nondescript spiritual lifetime until we bump into a fire extinguisher that tells us we better get ready because a really big fire is coming. Shouldn't the experiences of our lifetime somehow make a positive contribution to our continuing growth in grace? Isn't the journey also supposed to be memorable and full of Jesus?

Now, two years after that reflective moment at the end of the hallway, the La Sierra University church is caught up in a glorious project that will bring the corridor to life. Using multiple, framed four-by-eight-foot canvases to cover both sides of the corridor, the church envisions a captivating art project: an overview of the full Bible story, from Genesis to Revelation.

The art will portray not only details of the history and stories of Bible cultures and peoples but also the church's understanding of the Bible's teachings, ranging from the Creation, to the Sabbath, to the giving of the Ten Commandments and the Wilderness Sanctuary, through the pointed messages of the prophets, to the parables of Jesus, the establishment of the young Christian church, and the apocalyptic visions of the book of Revelation. The paintings will include all the colors, activities, characters, and animals of the biblical world, created to capture the imagination of children today. Yet it will also, in a realistic style, maintain the deep, devotional sense of awe the Bible so readily transmits to thoughtful adults.

La Sierra is also committed to presenting the Bible story both visually and in publications and Bible studies (which the staff will create to accompany the project) in a Christ-centered, grace-oriented manner. Every panel will point the viewer to Jesus. Every scene will assist in telling the gospel story of salvation by grace alone. In fact, the church is calling the project the Corridor of Grace.

THE ARTIST

The achievement of such a task requires the skill and commitment of an accomplished Christian artist. The La Sierra University church is privileged to have just such a person as a member of their church family—Elfred Lee, widely known throughout the Seventh-day Adventist Church for his published work, his dramatic depictions of the Christ of Revelation, and his grand murals found in institutional settings around the world. The church has secured Elfred's services for this project, discussed the concepts and purposes of the artwork with him, and watched him fall in love with the project. Three panels have already been produced and unveiled at the church, much to the congregation's delight. Two more panels are designed, drawn, and being painted at Elfred's studio. It takes three or four months to complete each panel.

To involve the congregation more intimately in the project, Elfred is using church members from all age categories and ethnic backgrounds as the models for his Bible characters. The stories chosen for the panels include ones of babies, children, teens, young adults, and older people, women and men, so that people of all ages will be able to find themselves in the Bible story. Ten couples from the church, long-time members of the congregation, appear as the ten patriarchal families at the end of panel number one, "The Eden Panel." Harold and Ruth Fagal are Abraham and Sarah in panel number two, "The Genesis Panel." On the same panel, you will recognize Jean Smith as Isaac's wife, Rebekah, helping Jacob steal his father's blessing. Pastors Dave Peckham, Janeen Little, and Dewald Kritzinger appear among the Israelites crossing the Red Sea on panel number four, "The Wilderness Panel," as do Corinne and Perry Campbell. Harold Lyle is Moses raising his staff over the parting sea and pointing the way out of Egypt. That's me, over there on panel number five, "The Kingdom Panel," being fed by ravens and listening to the still, small Voice.

Almost every character in the artwork reflects the face of a church member. Elfred costumes them and photographs them at the church, then paints their likenesses onto the canvases at his studio. Some day, many years from now, a mother will take her children into the corridor and say, "Look at panel number seven, 'The Bethlehem Panel.' Notice anything familiar about the Samaritan woman at the well who is talking to Jesus?"

The church refers to panel number eight as "The Central Panel." Here are depictions of Jesus in the climactic days of His ministry—calming the storm on Galilee, feeding the multitude, healing the blind man, entering Jerusalem. We see Him at the Last Supper. We witness His betrayal, His arrest, and His trials. The Crucifixion is pictured at the very center of the panel. The Resurrection and Christ's ascension into heaven happen to the right. It is the church's desire that everyone who looks at this art will understand the perspective that "the sacrifice of Christ as an atonement for sin is the great truth around which all other truths cluster. In order to be rightly understood and appreciated, every truth in the word of God, from Genesis to Revelation, must be studied in the light that streams from the cross of Calvary."[1] That's why the eighth of the ten panels is the *central* panel.

The church also has invested in new paint for the walls and new lighting for the corridor, chosen with the aid of the artist to highlight the panels in an optimum way. Ultimately, a brand-new hallway will emerge, with six panels going down the left side of the hallway, the Old Testament side, and four coming back, on the New Testament side. Church members continue to donate large and small amounts of money toward the completion of the project.

The La Sierra University church sees this Corridor of Grace as a magnificent introduction to the beliefs and practices of the Adventist family and a unique way of attracting people in the local community to the church. A grand opening will take place at the completion of the project, to which the church will invite community leaders, friends and neighbors, and, of course, the entire congregation. Newspaper and magazine articles will tell the story of how the paintings were envisioned and accomplished. The pastors imagine the children and youth of the church, in their baptismal classes, sitting in front of the pictures of the stories they are studying instead of sitting at a desk in the office complex. They see how others who are taking Bible studies will benefit from the scenes on the panels.

RESEARCH AND PLANNING

This huge undertaking already has taken

THE CORRIDOR OF GRACE

hundreds of hours of research, planning, and fine-tuning. Elfred has pored over dozens of books on biblical art. He traveled to the Holy Land, photographing the landscapes that will form the backgrounds to the panels. He has carefully noted local culture, dress, food, and flowers. He's done research in archaeological museums, studying ancient artifacts, including pots, weapons, and construction. The Tower of Babel in panel number two is patterned after depictions of Babylonian ziggurats. The pyramids in panels two and three are the actual pyramids at Saqqara and Giza in Egypt. The sheep with the stubby tails are the very type of sheep found in the Middle East. The Old Testament sanctuary is as faithful to the passages that tell its story as it can be painted. (Look closely, for example, at the ark of the covenant, and see, in the cutaway, the golden pot of manna, Aaron's rod that budded, and the Ten Commandments—with no Roman numerals!) The vessels to the side of the portrayal of the Last Supper are authentic first-century vessels. The boat on Galilee in panel eight is modeled on the fishing boat found at Tiberius—fondly referred to there as "the Jesus boat." The church wants the project to be as biblically accurate as it is artistically stunning.

Because it is situated directly beneath the church sanctuary, the Corridor of Grace will serve the La Sierra University church as a continuing reminder of the church's foundation in the teachings of the Bible. The artwork will be a constant reminder that the Christian's daily walk is more full of light and more joyful when it is grounded in the amazing Book we believe to be the Word of God. The corporate worship that takes place above the Corridor of Grace has come about because of the congregation's response to God's grace. The deepening sense of belonging to the family of faith is furthered because the church members understand community to be the way they reflect the grace of God to each other. When the church sends members on mission trips and community service projects and dedicates students as they leave for a year as student missionaries, it does so because it has found these activities to be effective ways of revealing God's grace to others.

And when the church invites people to visit, to attend meetings and concerts, lectures and seminars, this is the first place the members want to take them. Whenever people from the neighborhood want an answer to the question, "Who are the people who attend that big church on the corner of Sierra Vista and Pierce, and what do they believe?" church members

[155]

will walk with them down the steps and around the corner to the lower level of the church. They will turn on the lights to an inviting new hallway and walk in that light past ten beautiful, monumental pieces of art that portray the Bible story and describe the foundation for all we are, all we believe, all we do.

The identity of all of us as God's people, chosen by grace in Jesus before the creation of the world, is depicted in the art of the Corridor of Grace. All that God desires for His children—the forgiveness, adoption, and redemption freely given to us "in accordance with the riches of God's grace that he lavished on us with all wisdom and understanding"—will soon "be put into effect when the times will have reached their fulfillment—to bring all things in heaven and on earth together under one head, even Christ" (Ephesians 1:7, 8, 10).

How precious is the assurance of grace!

_____

1. White, *Gospel Workers,* 315.

NOTES

NOTES

NOTES

IF YOU'VE APPRECIATED THIS BOOK, YOU'LL WANT TO READ THESE OTHER THOUGHTFUL BOOKS BY ADVENTIST LEADERS.

The Promise of Peace
Charles Scriven

Too many Adventists have settled into a mind-numbing routine centering on an inherited lifestyle rather than on our Lord. Charles Scriven declares the Adventist vision in a manner that is at once practical and brief. Your life mission goes beyond family, church, and career. God's mission will take you on a path from common places to uncommon ones. There you may live by the promise of peace. And blessed you will be.
ISBN 10: 0-8163-2350-X

Beyond Common Ground
Alden Thompson

Q: Why do we have liberals and conservatives in our church?
A: Because Jesus needs them and so do we.

Alden Thompson shares his belief that the time has come to take Jesus' second command "You shall love your neighbor as yourself" and explore how liberals and conservatives can work together more effectively in our efforts to understand and apply God's Word in our lives. In the end, we will all be stronger, wiser, more patient, and more like God. That will mean great joy in heaven—and maybe more joy on earth.
ISBN 10: 0-8163-2340-2

A Life to Die For
W. Clarence and Stephen Schilt

Clarence as a pastor struggled to live the life he preached. Stephen as a psychiatrist was dominated primarily by a secular, humanistic agenda with spirituality having little relevance. The two of them were just surviving; one pursued spiritual reality, frustrated by the failure of his own efforts, one seeking the "good life," blissfully ignorant that it was an illusion. Although coming from radically different perspectives, both were mired in what they now call "dead living." Then they discovered "the life to die for." Allow this ultimate non-self-help book to radically change your life as it has so many others.
ISBN 10: 0-8163-2308-9

Three ways to order:

1 Local	Adventist Book Center®
2 Call	1-800-765-6955
3 Shop	AdventistBookCenter.com

Pacific Press®